Power
Schmoozing

Power
Schmoozing
The New Etiquette for Social and Business Success

Terri Mandell

McGraw-Hill
New York   San Francisco   Washington, D.C.   Auckland   Bogotá
Caracas   Lisbon   London   Madrid   Mexico City   Milan
Montreal   New Delhi   San Juan   Singapore
Sydney   Tokyo   Toronto

Library of Congress Cataloging-in-Publication Data

Mandell, Terri.
    Power schmoozing : the new etiquette for social and business
success / Terri Mandell—[Rev. ed.]
        p.   cm.
    ISBN 0-07-039887-9
    1. Public relations. 2. Business networks. 3. Social networks.
    4. Interpersonal relations. 5. Interpersonal communication.
    6. Success. I. Title.
HD59.M255 1996
650.1′3—dc20
                                        96-7871
                                         CIP

McGraw-Hill

*A Division of The **McGraw·Hill** Companies*

2 3 4 5 6 7 8 9 0 BKP/BKP 9 0 1 0 9 8 7

ISBN 0-07-039887-9

*The sponsoring editor for this book was Laura Friedman, the editing
supervisor was Jane Palmieri, and the production supervisor was
Donald Schmidt. It was set in Fairfield by Terry Leaden of McGraw-
Hill's Professional Book Group composition unit.*

Printed and bound by Quebecor/Book Press.

McGraw-Hill books are available at special quantity discounts to
use as premiums and sales promotions, or for use in corporate
training programs. For more information, please write to the
Director of Special Sales, McGraw-Hill, 11 West 19th Street, New
York, NY 10011. Or contact your local bookstore.

 This book is printed on recycled, acid-free paper containing a minimum of 50% recycled, de-inked fiber.

To Michael, Danny, and Georgi, my new family

Contents

Preface

During the 1980s, many of us between the ages of 25 and 45 were obsessed with establishing ourselves in the business world. The media called us "Yuppies," and our primary objective in life was to look good and get rich. The buzzword of the decade was networking, and my Power Schmoozing seminars were filled with aspiring young professionals looking for ways to connect with potential employers, clients, associates, and business-based friendships. They were bankers, entertainers, lawyers, consultants, hairdressers, therapists, and artists. Some were gainfully employed; others were desperate and broke. Their average age was about 35. They represented an equal split between males and females, and a wide range of ethnicities, nationalities, and world views.

It's been 6 years since the seminars began, and 4 years since the previous edition of this book was published. Things have changed. The demographic breakdown of the seminar students is the same, but the material is different. I used to talk about how to present your business card to hot prospects, and how to sell yourself to anyone who'd listen. I now focus primarily on how to tell the absolute truth about who you are in the first 5 minutes of a conversation. They don't teach that at the Harvard Business School.

Obviously, networking is still important, and the new edition still addresses schmoozing techniques and conversational strategies. As a businessperson, political activist, and tireless socializer, I'm always on the lookout for new contacts, and the Power Schmoozing techniques have proved their value over the years as I've attended business-based social functions, like gallery openings, awards banquets, groundbreaking ceremonies for shopping centers, and professional association meetings. I went to these events to look for new clients and other business connections, and I was good at it. But I soon realized that it was hard work, and there was probably a less stressful, less compromising, and more creative way to go about this business of networking.

Since the previous edition of this book, I've had a child (now 5 years old), gotten divorced, and married someone else. My life changed, the culture changed around me, and the Yuppie thing became a lot less important. I realized that contacts can be made at the car wash, at your kid's school, or on the street right in front of your own house. Opportunities for getting a life are everywhere. And that's what schmoozing is really about—getting a life.

The definition of sincerity is that you act the same with all people, all the time, rather than putting on a different face for different people. After talking to thousands of individuals about their emotional responses to meeting strangers, I can come to only one conclusion: that we're all dysfunctional. We're all living with an innate sense of unworthiness, and nothing challenges it more than meeting new people and wanting them to like us. We've been conditioned to mistrust strangers, and when we do let them get close to us, there's a constant, nagging fear that we won't measure up. Our etiquette training in this culture (and more so in others) has taught us to put on a facade for the world, and it's robbed us of the right to feel safe just being ourselves. That's why *Power Schmoozing* is about telling the absolute truth about who you are. After that, the business card, the follow-up, the sales pitch, and everything else just falls into place on its own.

So while the new *Power Schmoozing* will still give you great guidelines for getting ahead in business, it's also going to expand your thinking and help you do more than just build a career. Remember that our prime directive as humans is to seek out and make contact with one another, to form partnerships, groups, families, and communities. We're not just here to do business. We're here to make friends and find people to love. This is not optional. This is required.

But a sense of belonging in the world is hard to come by, and as long as we're etiquette victims operating on the old rules about how "nice boys and girls" should behave, it's going to be difficult to really connect with others. Think of *Power Schmoozing* as a course in etiquette recovery. Because networking, schmoozing, talking to anybody about anything, or whatever you want to call it, is more than just a technique for meeting influential, glamorous people and increasing your stature in the community. It's about believing in yourself and taking charge of your life, stopping all excuses for why your life isn't working, and instead, making your life into exactly what you want it to be.

Terri Mandell

Acknowledgments

Many thanks to many people.

To my dear friend Susan Roane. And to Laura Friedman at McGraw-Hill for taking a chance on making a small book into a big one.

As always, I thank all those who've ever attended a Power Schmoozing seminar, for the teachings they've given to me.

And to my soul mate Michael Jacobs, for showing up in my life and knowing how to tell the truth (and for taking Danny shopping for tools on Saturdays so I could write).

And thank you Jim, for a friendship with a value beyond measure.

Schmooze (shmōōz): *to chat idly or gossip.*

Power Schmoozing: *Aggressively and confidently connecting with others in order to create a more productive business and social life.*

Power
Schmoozing

Them and Us: Losing Your Fear of Strangers

Welcome to the intimidating social landscape of 1990s America. It's cold, overwhelming, and full of pretension, deceit, and scary monsters. Some of the monsters look a lot like us—they wear the same clothing, speak the same language, eat the same food, and see the same movies. But others don't look like us at all, and we've been taught to steer clear of them.

In this landscape there are two choices. You can either stay inside certain safe zones where you're already acquainted with some of the inhabitants, most of whom think, act, and look like you, or you can venture a little farther out, to where people may be less familiar, but much more intriguing. The farther out you go, the more interesting it gets. Each step outside the safety zone brings you closer to an expansive new view of the landscape. The payoff for going beyond the boundaries is that it also expands your view of yourself, by connecting you to other beings and *their* views. Ultimately, each of these connections has the potential to give you a gift; a new friend, a business contact, a lover, or a life. The challenge is: How do you get these individuals to notice you? To talk to you? To *like* you?

Sounds like an easy task for a capable, professional, articulate, easygoing individual like yourself, yes? Not really. Because there's something in the way. It's called the "them and us mentality," and most of us have been living with it since childhood.

Most of us learned about feeling separate from other human beings when we were little kids, at the same time we were learning to talk and think. Our parents may have taught us not to talk to strangers, or that the new family moving in down the block was "different" from us and, therefore, not quite safe to be around. When you were a child, you and your family formed a little group called "us." This group might have included aunts and uncles and extended family members, but anybody outside that group was "them." As you got a little older, "us" was expanded to include members of your community, which might have included your friends and the nice old guy who owned the corner store. But people outside that circle were still "them." Some of us were taught that anybody not a member of our race, nationality, or religion was "them." And others of us may have come to believe that anybody outside our gender or sexual orientation was also "them."

It's a lonely way to live, and unfortunately, many of our cultural myths perpetuate this thinking. In the 1980s, we got closer to dissolving those barriers when we started *networking*. Networking taught us to introduce ourselves to strangers, to start and maintain conversations, and to stay in touch with those strangers who interested us enough to become friends or associates. But the concept of networking for business is now overused, overhyped, and overexposed, and as we've gotten older, many of us have realized that the real idea is to make human connections of *any* kind. It's not just about business anymore—it's about *getting a life*. But the hard part of making those connections is, and has always been, having the guts to walk into a room full of strangers and *ask to be noticed*.

While we were kids being taught to fear strangers, we were also taught that it was impolite to draw attention to ourselves. Traditional rules of etiquette dictated that polite ladies and gentlemen (especially ladies) should be delicate and unassuming in the way they presented themselves. Expressing too much personality, speaking too directly or honestly to someone, or coming right out and asking for what we want was considered dangerous behavior. And it's that *anticipated* danger that stops us from feeling safe enough to really connect with other people. Networking, and in fact communicating in general, is a skill which has to be learned and cultivated, and it requires us to challenge our limitations and to rethink the way we behave. To do this, we have to cast out our notions about "them and us" and create a new view of the world as a safe place. The ability to feel secure in high-pressure social settings is something that all successful people have in common (even if they're just faking it).

But Why Bother?

Because human beings, and in fact all other animals, were not designed to live alone. Because life is better when we share it with others, when we're constantly adding new people and new friends to the mix. We learn about who we are by reflecting ourselves off other people. It's absolutely vital to survival, and to our emotional health. If these aren't good enough reasons for you, if you don't really care about your emotional health, or if these concepts are too lofty, then try schmoozing for a really simple reason: It's important to schmooze and connect with others because it's the best way to find a job or make business contacts, and we all have to earn money.

But the best reason of all is that you probably don't really want to spend every night of your life eating pizza alone in front of the TV, do you?

Working a Room

Take a good look around at the next party you attend. You'll notice that the people who are the most comfortable, the ones who are making the most of the social or business opportunities available and actually having fun doing it, are the ones who act *fearlessly*. They speak to strangers effortlessly, as if they were already acquainted. They always seem to say the right thing. They know everybody, or so it seems. And they have no shame about making sure their business cards get pressed into as many palms as possible.

If this behavior strikes you as a bit barracuda-like, perhaps you've had more than a few encounters with a pushy, loud-mouthed glad-hander who makes a fool of him- or herself by hitting on everybody in the room for something, be it business leads or mating possibilities. You know the stereotype—the sleazoids who cruise the party looking for victims to manipulate into a crooked business deal or a meaningless sexual encounter. It's unfortunate that these poor types never learned how to sell themselves more delicately, because there really can be a great deal of dignity in aggressive socializing when it's done properly. Unfortunately, this art isn't really taught anywhere, so many of us have ended up with a negative image of "working a room" that's more mythical than real.

Knowing how to effectively work a room is only the first in a series of steps that can lead to a life filled with new, interesting people and limitless creative possibilities. It's an exercise in breaking free of "them and us" mentality. And it's an ongoing activity. It doesn't promise instant gratification, because it's designed to bring new people into your *future*. It requires a long-term view, strategic planning, and a commitment to working at it—every day. Not only does it mean knowing how to find the right places to go, the right people to talk to when you get there, and the right angle on the conversation; it also means that you take the primary responsibility for the development of the relationship over the months and years that follow the first contact. And you can't do that if you're afraid of strangers.

The Best Social Events in Town, and How to Find Them

Whether you're mingling for business or social purposes, you can find a wealth of events that attract exactly the kinds of people you're looking for every day and night of the week by beginning somewhere as simple as your local newspaper.

On a daily or weekly basis, most newspapers publish a calendar-of-events section which lists a variety of activities, from nature hikes to black-tie dinners for charities. Most cities and small towns have their own weekly or monthly publications, and many of them are free (like the *L.A. Weekly* or the *Chicago Reader*). Cities and states also publish magazines like *Monterey Life, New Jersey Monthly, South Florida Living,* and *Oregon Coast,* and almost all of them feature a calendar of events, listing everything from volleyball tournaments to support groups for single parents. These are excellent, ready-made, up-to-date sources for entertainment, cultural, community, and other social events. In the business world, you can find events by perusing local business magazines like the *San Jose Business Journal* and *Miami Business Today,* which list seminars, professional association luncheons, charity events, and community meetings.

If you're not in the habit of attending rallies for your favorite political cause or lectures about your community's historic architecture, then you've been missing out on a world of opportunities to meet people who share your interests. These very public, yet very anonymous gatherings provide a safe, nonintimidating environment in which to connect with others, and they can keep your social calendar filled for weeks on end. The best part is, at events like this, everybody in the room is focused on a specific topic, so you'll always have something to talk about.

In some cities, the Chamber of Commerce can refer you to directories which list important local events. Los Angeles has a monthly directory available by subscription called the *L.A. Master Planner,* which is updated monthly and lists social, civic, charitable, entertainment, and professional events for the coming 12 months. Call your city's Convention and Visitors Bureau and ask if a similar directory exists. If you find one, *use it*. Go through it each month with a highlighting pen, and choose events that will provide the best opportunities to meet the people you're looking for.

In Los Angeles, a city of 8 million people, I lose patience with my single friends who lament that there's no place to go to meet people. With due respect for the misery of life alone in a big city and the cold, impersonal nature of it all, there are millions of people taking up space out there, and every one of them has some kind of interest, hobby, or occupation that could serve as a bridge to link them to you. Look for those bridges, and you'll find interesting, open, attentive people waiting for you on the other side. The more you do this, the less everybody will look like "them."

Your Identity: How to Find It, and How to Use It

Assuming you've summoned the energy to attend one of these events, and you've zeroed in on a person or persons you'd like to meet, how do you approach them? What do you say? How do you find the common thread?

After hellos are exchanged, the standard conversation starter at business events is generally to ask someone what business he or she is in. This question is usually posed as "What do you do?" and can be answered in one of two ways: either by giving your job description (stockbroker, teacher, writer, parent) or by taking the question at face value, answering it in any way you choose (I'm unemployed and I spend my days watching reruns of the Waltons). Defining someone by what they do for a living is very "them and us." It perpetuates the idea that people should be judged by their professional status. When you ask "What do you do?" people will reply by giving their job titles, rather than describing the other elements that make them unique individuals. For some of us, a job description ("I'm an entertainment attorney") may be all the information we need—or want—to volunteer about ourselves. But for those of us who may not be in such a glamorous and self-defining profession, a job title may present an inaccurate and limited picture of who we are. Next time you want to know more about someone, try asking a different way. "What's your story?" is one of my favorites.

If you're making a living as a house painter while working on a brilliant invention that you hope to market someday, would you call yourself a house painter or an inventor? Tradition dictates that when someone asks "What do you do?" it really means "What are you *paid* to do?" This assumption can make people uncomfortable, because they may not be proud of the work they're doing to earn a living. Some of us are flipping burgers or driving taxis while we're writing a novel or going to nursing school at night. Yet we're under the mistaken notion that we have to answer by giving a job description.

Take a moment to look at yourself and the things you care about. Look at the things you do "on the side." (A terrible expression! As if your job is your only identity, and all other things that define you are placed somewhere adjacent to your life rather than playing any real part in it.) Are you a cellular phone salesman with an interest in holistic medicine? Or a high school teacher who's also a wine collector? Maybe you work as a clerk in a supermarket, but you enjoy motorcycle racing on the weekends. Or ballet. Or growing prize-winning roses. The choice about how to define yourself and how to express that to other people is *yours*. There are more facets to who you are than you may be aware of, and each one has a potential audience and peer group. All you have to do is to *let them know you're there*.

Suppose you have a passion for photography. You shoot pictures and work in your darkroom every chance you get. Your work is good, but you're not a professional—yet. In fact, you make your living as a bank teller. But if becoming a professional photographer is an important dream of yours, and you can't wait to ditch that boring bank job, then there are two things you can do. Either you can spend your time feeling depressed and frustrated because you're stuck with your day job or you can start creating an agenda for Power Schmoozing with people who can help you attain your goal. In this book, we're going to assume that you've chosen the latter, and that you're ready to move into a state of action instead of a state of frustration.

The next time you're in a part of town where there's a gallery with a photo exhibit, stop in and take a look around. While you're there, add your name to the gallery's mailing list. Chat with the owner. Ask if he or she knows of related events or workshops going on. Now do the same with the other galleries in town. Call or visit them and get on their mailing lists. In a few weeks, you'll start to receive invitations to openings of new exhibits, receptions for artists, and nature hikes led by an outdoor photography teacher. Then, instead of throwing those invitations in the trash because you feel as though you're not really part of that crowd and wouldn't know how to act once you got there, *force yourself to go.* Bring a friend along for a sense of security if you need to.

You'll find yourself with a group of people who share your interests (or perhaps your business ideas) regarding photography. And since you have some knowledge in this area, you'll have something to talk about. Improve your odds for success by doing some preliminary research, like reading up on the latest technical advances or calling the gallery in advance to ask for some information about the artist. This way, not only will you arrive well informed, you'll already have a relationship with the gallery owner who spoke to you on the phone.

This approach works for anyone with a definable interest. Are you a marine biologist? If you're active in your field, you probably attend conventions, conferences, or awards banquets. How about stretching your horizons a bit and attending a conference that focuses on a different but related area, like environmental protection? Perhaps you have some knowledge or special ability you can offer to an environmental group on a volunteer basis. Think of all the new and interesting people, ideas, or business opportunities you might discover when you start analyzing sea water samples for Greenpeace. With all your expertise, you could end up on the evening news as a spokesperson for environmentalists when the next oil spill occurs. That's not a far-fetched notion. That's the way it really happens.

Whatever your interests are, there is a group or organization somewhere dedicated to them, and finding that group is easier than you think.

After you've taken some time to look through the newspaper and trade magazine event listings, take a trip to your local library and ask to see a remarkable reference source called the *Encyclopedia of Associations*. It's a massive directory which lists every business, social, political, and special-interest group in the United States, organized by category and key words. In addition to the mainstream business organizations like the Academy of Family Physicians, the Building Industry Association, and Pest Control Operators of America, you can also find hobby and sports-related groups like the Falcon Club and the Alaska Handball Association. All the major national associations are listed, such as the Heart Association and the Humane Society, as well as less mainstream groups, like the Jazz Society of the Desert and the Colorado Peace Network. There's even a Foreign Car Haters Club of America, a Black Lesbian Poets Society, and a San Diego Jitterbug Club. You get the idea.

Once you find the groups you like, call or write to them and ask to be put on their mailing lists. It usually isn't necessary to join. They'll send you information about programs and events in your area, and after you've attended a few meetings or lectures, you might decide you like the group enough to become a member. But in the meantime, you've plugged yourself into an abundant source of potential new friends and business contacts. And an instant social life.

Developing a Sense of Belonging

Can't afford a $500 ticket to the Save the Rain Forest fundraiser next month? Or maybe you can, but would you still feel awkward walking into a room full of wealthy socialites, none of whom you're acquainted with?

Glamorous charity events are one of the best forums for meeting and schmoozing with influential people, and one of the rare places where you might have a friendly conversation with a famous celebrity or industrial tycoon. But there's one small problem. Most of us can't afford the admission price, and even if we could, parties like these can be intimidating to someone who's just learning to hone his or her socializing skills.

Don't despair. There is a way to be welcomed without paying, and to feel much more secure and in control during the event—become a volunteer!

Volunteering connects you to entire new worlds to which you never thought you'd have access. It allows you to get closer to the people in the group. It gives you a "job" at the event, a reason for being there so that you won't feel a need to explain yourself. It gives you something to do instead of just standing around waiting for something to happen. And being part of the committee or group that hosts the event puts you in a position of authority, which will draw people to you for information and conversation. But most important, it will make you feel like you belong, which does wonders for your confidence, and gives you a real head start in making contact with others.

Let's assume that you've found an organization you enjoy, be it business-oriented, political, or charitable. It doesn't need to be a high-visibility group that attracts movie stars and media attention. It can be a local church group that distributes clothing to the homeless, or a hospital guild that raises funds for research. Almost all these groups rely on donations to survive, and they collect these donations by holding fundraising events.

The most effective way to acquire a sense of belonging is to *become active in the group*. The benefits are enormous. If you volunteer to serve on the committee that plans the fundraising dinner, you can often expect to attend without having to purchase a ticket. If you're on the committee that contacts people by phone to tell them about the dinner (or the seminar, or the building dedication), you're going to "know" a lot of them when they show up at the event, because you've spoken with them on the phone. At the same time, you've had a chance to get to know your coworkers on the committee, which gives you instant access to them and to *their* friends and contacts.

Let me give an example from my personal experience. Several years ago I was asked by a friend in the public relations business to join a committee which raised funds for an organization that helped homeless families. I was reluctant, primarily because it required that I attend weekly meetings at 8 a.m., and secondarily because I figured I was way too busy to take on any new projects. But I forced myself to get involved because the other members of the group were well-connected professionals, and I knew how valuable the networking opportunities would be. I dragged myself to the weekly meetings, and found that all I needed to contribute was enough time to make a few phone calls and write a press release once a month. Easy. And I was really helping to make a difference in my community.

I served on that committee for 2 years, and during that time we produced fund-raising dinners, art auctions, bowling tournaments, and other events which attracted celebrities, political leaders, and other VIPs. We raised hundreds of thousands of dollars for the organization. And in the process, I was able to rub shoulders with people to whom I would normally have no access. I schmoozed with some of the biggest stars in Hollywood, like Whoopi Goldberg and George Burns. And I learned and devised the basic building blocks of Power Schmoozing.

So I cannot emphasize strongly enough the importance and the effectiveness of using volunteering for groups and committees as a tool for marketing yourself. There's the obvious satisfaction that comes from helping others, and with it, a chance to help yourself.

Committees that schedule speakers are always a good bet. If you can become involved in the process of inviting guest speakers to your organization's luncheons, workshops, or special events, you'll be able to reach the real VIPs. Not just the attendees, but the people whom the group considers special. For instance, you might end up escorting the speaker to the event, picking her up at the airport, working on the publicity surrounding her appearance, or taking her to dinner.

There are other, less time-consuming ways to volunteer as well. If you're the person who checks off people's names at the door for instance, you'll have a chance to personally greet everyone who walks into the room. If guests will be required to wear name tags (which is always a good idea), then you'll have a chance to check out their credentials and affiliations as well. Name tags should ideally have a space to write in "company," or "affiliation" so everyone can get a better idea of whom they're talking to. The idea is to become a part of the event as opposed to a spectator.

In Susan RoAne's marvelous book *How to Work a Room*, she talks about something she calls "host versus guest mentality," which means that when you arrive at an event, you shouldn't act like a guest, waiting to be taken care of. Instead, act like a host, greeting people, creating goodwill, bringing people together, and taking responsibility for the way you experience the event. Ordinarily, you wouldn't consider taking over as host at another person's party by greeting guests, taking their coats, or offering them refreshments. But at a very large gathering, your help in this area could be very valuable to the real host. Try it sometime. You'll be amazed at the results.

And speaking of hosts, whenever you arrive at an event where you know nobody in the room, the most important person you can introduce yourself to is the host. It's her job to make sure everyone has a good time, and if you let her know that this is your first time attending one of these functions and that you don't know anybody yet, she'll take care of you. She'll know who the real movers and shakers are in the group, and will usually be delighted to introduce you to them. But if you don't let her know you're there, she won't be able to help you out. So don't be afraid to speak up. There are people in that room who want to meet you as much as you want to meet them.

The bottom line, of course, is that you have to take action. It can be a frightening first step to suddenly decide that starting today, you're going to make your presence known to the world. But the long-term benefits of intentionally creating a social life for yourself are immeasurable. Imagine how your life would be different if you could meet two or three new people each month. And what would it be like if at least one of those people brought you a new possibility for your future, such as a business lead, an exciting adventure, a romantic encounter, or an introduction to another new friend?

Taking these first small steps is going to require a lot from you. You'll have to break some of the rules that you always considered nonnegotiable—like the ones that say you're supposed to be humble, nonintrusive, and self-effacing. From this moment on, we're going to abandon those ideas, and instead of being well-behaved children who've learned how to be seen and not heard, we're now going to be interesting, confident adults learning how to create the lives that we want.

Communicating:
A New Set of Rules

The most important guidelines for communicating successfully and on your own terms are:

- Tell the truth.
- Take risks.
- Tell your whole story.
- Break rules.

Tell the truth? What kind of rule is that?

Show Up and Tell Your Whole Story

I'm willing to bet that very few of us were taught as children
that telling the truth was an important code to live by. Instead,
most of us were raised to believe that the ability to cover up
the truth gracefully was a much more valuable asset in terms
of getting ahead in the world.

Admitting that you don't know something—or asking a
question when it's presumed you already know the answer—is
one way of telling the truth. Other kinds of truth might
involve admitting that you're shy, or that you're new in town
and you're having a hard time meeting new people, or that
you're prospecting for new clients, a prospective spouse, or a
new job. I'm not advocating *brutal* honesty—you don't have to

15

tell people your true age or real hair color (although if you're really living in the truth there's no reason not to)—I'm advocating the kind of truth that comes from believing that contrary to what we were taught as children, we *are* allowed to reveal ourselves to others.

Many of us have been in situations where we were embarrassed to admit we didn't know something. So we tried to cover up for it, making excuses, or pretending we knew the answer when we really didn't, only to find that we were digging ourselves into an ever deepening cover-up. Why do we do this? Because we believe it's better to save face than to show our true face, and that telling the truth, admitting to a mistake or to ignorance about something, is a last resort. Here's my favorite story about what happens when we try to cover up instead of telling the truth.

Carrie, who worked for the Microsoft Corporation, was an ambitious, bright, and extremely personable woman in her thirties who intended to make it to the top—fast. One evening, she had the good fortune to have been invited to an important company dinner for top executives at Microsoft. The guest of honor was to be none other than Bill Gates, founder of the company, and one of the most admired (and richest) entrepreneurs in America. Gates is a very important guy, and was a great hero of hers, partly because she believed so strongly in the company, and partly because she was trying so hard to get ahead. She looked forward to meeting him so that she could impress him with her advanced understanding of the company and its products.

After dinner her big moment finally arrived. Her boss took her over to Gates and introduced her, complete with fanfare about how talented she was, how she had transformed her department and saved the company millions of dollars, and on and on. Gates, quite interested, smiled, shook her hand, and asked her a question about one of her current projects. The question was simple, and though she knew the answer as well as she knew her own name, her mind suddenly went blank. She was star-struck, and nervous about whether she'd say "the right thing." Beginning to panic, and trying her best to compose herself, she couldn't think of one intelligent thing to say.

Her nervousness about meeting him and her need to make an impression got the best of her, and she fumbled clumsily with her words, trying to cover up the fact that she didn't have the answer. Gates looked at her quizzically, and with amusement, waiting for her to pull herself out of the mess she was creating. As she tells it, the conversation never recovered, but withered and died right there on the spot, leaving her completely humiliated and apologizing, which made the situation even worse. Not only had she blown the opportunity she'd so looked forward to, but she had walked away from it hating herself.

After Carrie finished telling me this story, she asked me, "What should I have done?"

The answer is simple, obvious, and unexpected. *She should have told the truth.*

Rerun this scene in your mind (as no doubt Carrie has a couple of hundred times) and imagine that instead of trying to cover up, she had laughed and said something like, "You know, Bill, I've got to admit that I was kind of nervous about meeting you because I really wanted to impress you, and even though I know the answer to the question you just asked me, my mind has just gone blank, and I can't remember what it is. How embarrassing. Ask me something else."

How natural! And so disarming. So human.

Both of them would have gotten a good laugh out of that, and the ice would have been broken immediately. By telling the truth, Carrie would have enabled them to both step out of their roles for a moment—his being the all-powerful guru, and hers being the lowly devotee hoping to touch the hem of his garment. She would have also been *telling her whole story,* which would have given him more information about her, enough to help *him* contribute something to the conversation so that she didn't have to do all the work. In the old movies, her words would have been so honest and pure that he would have found her irresistibly charming, and they would have fallen in love and walked off into the sunset together. In real life, being that straight with people has the same effect. It can be so refreshing, that people actually *will* fall in love with you.

My generation—and probably yours—grew up believing that being polite meant speaking softly and unobtrusively, not asking direct questions, not talking about our personal lives, and drawing as little attention to ourselves as possible. In other words, we were taught to be good little girls and boys. Seen and not heard. Invisible.

As a result, many of us grew up living in a cocoon, where nobody was allowed in and our real selves were strictly controlled and certainly not allowed out. *Telling the truth, taking risks, telling our whole stories*, and *breaking rules* are some of the tools we can use to help free ourselves from that conditioning. In Chapter 5, which deals with fear, we'll look at how some of the traditional rules of polite behavior have rendered us incapable of asking for what we want. But in this chapter, I'm going to give you some very specific techniques for talking honestly to people, and for making those moments of contact more meaningful.

Eye Contact

Eye contact is the single most important, influential, and responsible type of communication in the universe, and that applies to all life forms, from CEOs of international conglomerates to aliens from Mars. Its power is that universal. Try it sometime with your dog. Or a little baby. Or a teenager. Then go out into the world and start using it with everybody else. And notice how the quality of your conversation improves.

You may be the most attractive person in the room, with an arsenal of the best opening lines. But if you can't look someone in the eye, you're going to have a hard time appearing sincere and interested in what people are saying to you. I'm not talking about a glancing quickly in the direction of someone's eyes and then letting your gaze wander from here to there with an occasional look back to the face. I'm talking about making yourself really available to someone. And in the process, creating a mind-lock with everyone and anyone you care about.

Because eye contact is so powerful, it can also be very frightening for some people because it leaves them no place to hide. You'll notice that people who are being less than honest, or who are very insecure, won't be able to look into anyone's eyes for very long. But if you're truly ready to be contacted, then you should have nothing to hide.

When you use steady eye contact to lock onto someone during a conversation, you can try a few interesting experiments. Notice how the strong people will play along with you, holding your gaze as deeply as you hold theirs. You can almost hear them thinking, "Ah, this person is a heavy hitter. I'll show her that I am too." You begin to feel the energy level rise, and you can bet that this is going to be a stimulating exchange.

But what if you've engaged a shy person whose eyes wander everywhere except to the vicinity of yours? Try to gently focus on his eyes, and win his trust by remaining there in an open, inviting way, not a challenging one. But don't stare him down—you don't want to terrorize the poor guy. Give him a break and look away once in a while. Also, remember that someone who is shy—and makes it apparent by not being able to look into your eyes—should be respected, even though his lack of focus may be a personal turn-off to you.

In addition to making conversations-in-progress more meaningful and more honest, eye contact is the best tool to use when trying to start a conversation from scratch. If you're in a room and spot someone you'd like to talk to, simply catch her eye and hold it there for an extra microsecond before you smile and say hello (a proven flirting trick). Two things can happen when you do this. One, you'll establish a bit of a connection before the first word is spoken. And two, if you're not completely comfortable about issuing the first hello, holding that person's gaze just a little longer than normal will often force her to say hello first, because she'll feel that something is expected of her. Try this next time you're standing in a crowded elevator where no one is talking to anyone else.

Opening Lines: Creating Common Ground

Opening lines are not as difficult as many people think because whenever you're in the same room with someone, you immediately have several things in common. If you base your opening lines on the *reality you're both sharing at the moment*, you'll soon be on your way to a real conversation.

For example, if you're at a fund-raiser for AIDS research, and a well-known entertainer is scheduled to perform later in the evening, you have two instant subjects for sharing. "Hi. How are you?" (Answer: "Fine, and you?") "Isn't it great that Sammy Smith and his Orchestra are playing tonight? I've always loved big bands."

Now you've started something. Maybe your prospect hates Sammy Smith. How interesting! Why? Or maybe she turns out to be an old friend of Sammy's, from Seattle.

YOU: Seattle? I was there for a convention just last month. I love the new shopping mall downtown.

SHE: I've never seen it. I haven't been there in years.

YOU: It's a great town. Did you know that public transportation downtown is *free*? It's really a city that works.

At this point, your prospect is either going to perk up and participate in the conversation or not. Maybe she's interested in city planning. Or Seattle. If not, she might have something to say about Sammy Smith. Or about AIDS (remember, you're both there for the fund-raiser). You've now introduced several topics, and hopefully your prospect will pick up on at least one of them. You can help the conversation along by creating new segues until she responds.

But remember that you can lead someone only so far. If

you've had the misfortune to have latched onto a dud, or if the chemistry just isn't there, or if she's preoccupied with something else and isn't in the mood for socializing, you may need to move on to someone else and begin again. Just remind yourself not to take her indifference as a personal rejection. She's got baggage of her own that she's brought into the room with her. Perhaps she just had a fight with her husband, or lost a big account, or was involved in a fender-bender on her way to the party. It's possible that she's terribly shy, depressed, or socially inept for a variety of reasons that have to do with her own personal history and nothing whatsoever to do with you. It's not your job to win her over, to heal her, or to take responsibility for her state of mind. Concentrate instead on taking responsibility for your own.

What if you've never been to Seattle? Or you've never heard of Sammy Smith? And you know nothing about city planning? *Remember that you're still occupying a common reality.* The very fact that you're in the same room for the same event gives you something to talk about.

Let's say you're a building contractor who's always worked in residential construction, and you now want to move into commercial construction. You go to a meeting of the Downtown Development Association, where the big-time developers congregate. You see an interesting, successful-looking person standing alone, so you gradually move closer until you're standing right alongside him. You establish eye contact, and:

YOU: Hi, How are you doing? My name's Harvey.

HE: Hello. I'm Albert.

YOU: Nice to meet you, Albert. Are you a member of this organization?

HE: No, but I come to these meetings sometimes. How about you?

YOU: I'm not a member either. But I like coming to these meetings to find out what's going on with the 8th Street development project. I'm a building contractor.

This is typical of the conversations and introductions that occur at a lot of business or community functions. Most people will respond to you if you approach them with a simple "Hi." In this case, you've told Albert your name and that you're a building contractor. That's the beginning of *your whole story.* The more you reveal about yourself, the more the other person will reveal. Your honesty, your ability to volunteer information about who you are, what you do, why you're there, or what you're looking for, helps make the other person feel safe about doing the same. The more you contribute to a conversation like this, the more you'll get in return.

Chances are if Albert is at the Downtown Development Association meeting, he's probably in a field related to yours, so there are dozens of subjects you can address. Like how the mayor takes bribes from crooked real estate developers (careful, though—he may be one of them). Or how the water shortage affects the construction industry. You just have to take the initiative, create opportunities to connect one subject to another, and learn when to quit if your presentation isn't working.

It's really not so much about knowing the best opening lines as it is about being observant, and commenting on what you observe. You might find yourself at your cousin's wedding standing next to someone who's munching on a 3000-calorie cheesecake puff from the buffet table. Why not say, "Aren't these 3000-calorie cheesecake puffs incredible?" No doubt your prospect will respond in an equally lighthearted manner. From there, see where you can take it. Maybe, "I don't eat this stuff in real life," or "I heard that this caterer was just hired to do a dinner at the White House," and so on, until you're comfortable enough to move into something a little more serious, like, "Are you a friend of the bride or the groom?"

Here then, are some other opening lines, based on observing a shared reality:

1. Wasn't the traffic out there horrendous?

2. The speaker tonight was brilliant (boring, fascinating, opinionated).
3. Isn't this hotel gorgeous? My father knew the architect.
4. Nice jacket.
5. It's always so amusing to watch a bunch of lawyers work a room, isn't it?

Targeting Specific Individuals

What if you want to approach someone you've heard about, but don't know personally? For many people, that can be a frightening prospect. But in reality, it can be much easier because you already know something about the person you want to meet. Armed with that information, you can easily go beyond a two-word greeting and say, "Hello, Dr. Riley. I read about the award you received for your research on the relationship between cholesterol levels and athletic performance. I'm really impressed with your work. I've been working on a similar research project myself."

If we look at this opener for a minute, we can see all the most effective elements at work. By introducing yourself to Dr. Riley this way, you've done the following:

1. Taken a risk ("Hello, Dr. Riley.")
2. Communicated ("I read about the award you received.")
3. Told the truth ("I'm impressed with your work.")
4. Told your whole story ("I'm working on a similar project.")

In this conversation, you've given Dr. Riley a lot to work with. You've made it easy for him to respond by serving up several tidbits on which he can comment, and by showing him that you can communicate and are willing to share yourself. *He knows that he won't be expected to do all the work in a conversation with you.* Nine times out of ten, Dr. Riley will be interested in hearing about your project—particularly if you've done your homework and you're truly familiar with his work and your chosen subject.

Never underestimate the power of being prepared. Read the trade publications associated with your profession, the newspapers, the gossip columns, and anything else you can find that will help you arm yourself with information. Better yet, if you've chosen your target prior to the event, and you have access to information about him, come prepared with two or three topics that you may have in common. ("I heard you fly a Cessna 210. I once flew in one and loved the view without the struts in the way.")

*   *   *   *   *

Tips for Engaging People in Interesting Conversations

1. Open by commenting on any shared reality you can find: "Are you a member of this group?" "Isn't the bride beautiful?" "Can you believe the smog today?"

2. Use multilayered sentences whenever possible, and try to end with a question. Example: "No, I'm not a member, but I'm interested in their work and I have a friend who's a member. She said it was a great group with good networking opportunities, so I thought I'd check it out. How about you?"

3. Remember to contribute substance to the conversation as opposed to making the other person do all the work. A common mistake in first conversations is to fire off one question after another, turning it into a one-sided and ultimately uncomfortable interview.

4. Tell the truth and tell your whole story. "I'm newly divorced and it's really lonely out there. I'm trying to meet as many new people as I can." Or, "I'm a cement contractor trying to expand my business, so I'm here to meet real estate developers who might be able to throw some work my way."

5. Maintain a sense of humor. "I took a self-improvement seminar that gave us a homework assignment to meet three new people this month, and you're number three!" (Also a nice way of telling the truth.)

6. Create an opportunity for a second encounter or conversation. You don't have to close a deal on the spot. Just create an *on ramp*, which you can complete later on in the party, or on another day.

7. Get to the point:

> SHE: ...so after we introduce our new soft-drink product into the marketplace, we're going to start producing nonalcoholic beer.
>
> YOU: Really? I worked on the radio campaign for Blarto Beer last year. I've done a lot of new product introductions in the beverage market.

8. Let the other person complete his or her story. Don't interject information about yourself in the middle of someone else's dialogue. Here's an example:

> HIM: My wife and I went to France this year...
>
> YOU: Oh, I was there in 1991. We went to all the museums, and drank a lot of wine.
>
> HIM: Well, anyway, we took the kids with us, and my little boy...
>
> YOU: We left our kids at home. I didn't want to spend the money for their airfare.
>
> HIM: Oh, that's nice. Anyway, my son got the flu on the plane...
>
> YOU: Oh, I had the flu last week; it was terrible. I should have gotten a flu shot.
>
> HIM: Uh huh. Well, look at the time. I have to go now.

9. Beware of verbal styles that make you look insecure, such as:

   - Uptalking—when the words at the end of your sentences fly "up" so that everything you say sounds like a question (My name's Terri? I'm a nurse? I live in Encino?)

- Name dropping—mentioning the names of all the famous and important people you know is a huge turnoff. Don't do it.
- Saying "uh" all the time—make a tape recording of yourself talking on the phone to see if it sounds like this, "Hello. Uh. This is, uh, Steve Sanford calling. Uh, I'm looking for John Merrick. I'm, uh, returning his call."
- Saying "you know" all the time—self-explanatory. It's a lot like "uh."
- Mumbling or speaking too softly.

As you practice your new skills, pay attention to how they're working. Review your various encounters in your mind, and consider the following questions. The answers will surprise, educate, and enlighten you!

*   *   *   *   *

*   *   *   *   *

Things to Observe in Yourself and Others

1. Where would telling the truth have worked better than what you actually said?
2. What did you notice about the other person's body language? And your own?
3. Was anything said that might have sounded like a sexual come-on (if it wasn't intended to)?
4. Was there humor and disarmament in the conversation?
5. Was the person comfortable being him- or herself?
6. Were you?

*   *   *   *   *

Escaping Unwanted Conversations

What if someone very unappealing corners you, bores you with stories about his performing dog, shows you endless pictures of his kids, has bad breath, and doesn't have one really interesting thing to say? Or what if it's someone who looks interesting at first, but turns *un*interesting fast? What if she bores you to distraction, or has nothing to offer, and you could spend your time more productively with someone else? How do you escape?

As is the case with all communicating, telling the truth should always be your first choice. (You can't beat the direct approach, especially when there's a good chance you'll get caught if you lie.) So try playing it this way: Reach out to shake the person's hand and say, "It's been nice talking to you, Eugene. Good luck with your dog tricks, they're really great! I'm going to go work the room a little more right now. Maybe I'll catch up with you later."

That's *total honesty.* And not offensive in the least, because it's understood that the reason everyone is there is to meet one another. Remember, working the room is an acceptable excuse for moving on.

If you want to make your exit a little less abrupt, you can offer some sort of connecting gesture, like a handshake or a pat on the arm or shoulder. This gives the subtle message that you like Eugene enough to touch him, and it softens the blow of the abandonment. Now, Eugene, if he is well versed in the ways of the world, not only will understand your reason for leaving him, but will respect you for it, and he'll let you go.

Then there are the times when you've hooked up with someone who isn't quite so sophisticated. Maybe he's had a really bad day, and has an inferiority complex to boot, and your departure at that moment reminds him of how his father abandoned him when he was 5, how all his girlfriends left him, how he gets fired from all his jobs, how nobody likes him—and now you've gone and done the same thing to him all over again.

Well, whose problem is that?

You have a clear choice here. You can either let him take responsibility for his own reality or spend the evening *taking care of him,* making sure you don't hurt his feelings, while you miss all the other opportunities in the room. If you choose the latter, no wonder you always leave the party unsatisfied! Some of us live our whole lives this way, taking better care of others than of ourselves. Then we wonder why our lives don't work.

If you see no other way but to lie, then do it with a little grace. You can simply use the old line, "Excuse me. I see someone across the room whom I need to speak with before she leaves." Exits like that can get a little complicated if there's really no one for you to actually go and talk to. The person you've just left may watch you go. And while it isn't your responsibility to take care of that person's feelings, even little lies can accelerate into big dramas and tarnished reputations. That's why honesty is always more effective.

Working with a Partner

Another escape tactic requires a partner. If you're schmoozing with a friend, you can establish a set of signals that will work in a tight situation. My ex-husband, Jim, and I invented a couple of moves that we used successfully for years. One of them goes like this:

I'm talking to someone from whom I wish to escape, and Jim joins us. To indicate my desire to be rescued, I reach behind his back or across his shoulder as I'm introducing him. It looks like I'm putting my arm around him, but what I'm really doing is tapping him three times, which means, "Kindly get us out of here." He knows this signal, and responds by coming up with a line like, "I'm glad I found you, Terri. Can I speak to you for a minute?" Or, "We should call Mr. Jones in New York before 9 o'clock." Or, "We need to say good-bye to Paula. She's about to leave the party." It makes for a smooth and graceful exit every time.

Another powerful partner trick Jim and I invented addresses the problem of forgotten names. When someone I know comes up to say hello and I can't remember her name, I try to be honest, apologizing for the fact that it's mysteriously escaped me at the moment. This works well with distant acquaintances or business contacts. But it's quite embarrassing to forget the name of someone you're trying to impress, like a new client. The solution, when your partner is with you, is to play this game:

The person approaches and says hello. We greet each other warmly, and I then indicate my partner and say to the person, "This is my husband, Jim." Jim knows that when I introduce him this way, *without mentioning the other person's name*, it means that I've forgotten it. So he covers for me by immediately saying, "Nice to meet you. And you are...?" The person will introduce herself to *him*, thereby revealing her identity to both of us.

This technique requires advance planning with your partner, and an established set of signals that more or less remains constant. Experiment and see what works best for you.

There's only one thing that really works when it comes to communication: being yourself. But in order to *become* yourself, you often have to go against the grain. With practice, you'll be shocked to learn how simple it can be to *tell the truth, take risks, tell your whole story*, and *break rules*. Read on.

*   *   *   *   *

Old vs. New Rules

Then

1. Don't talk to strangers.
2. Don't eavesdrop on conversations.
3. Don't interrupt.
4. Don't brag about your accomplishments.
5. Speak softly.
6. Always think of others before yourself.
7. Accept compliments reluctantly.
8. Don't tell family secrets.
9. Don't admit when you don't know something.

10. Don't be *different*.
11. Don't accept food or drink when it's first offered.
12. Keep your opinions to yourself.
13. Life isn't fun.
14. Be stable.

Now

1. Talk to everyone, everywhere, about everything.
2. Listen in on other people's conversations.
3. Break in on other people's conversations.
4. Tell your whole story.
5. Speak with confidence.
6. Take care of yourself before taking care of others.
7. Accept compliments. You deserve them.
8. Support common ground whenever you find it.
9. Ask questions. Be vulnerable.
10. Be yourself.
11. Accept what you want. Decline what you don't.
12. Have an opinion. Have a personality.
13. Life isn't anything. You create it as you go along.
14. Be yourself.

*   *   *   *   *

Where to Go,
What to Do,
Who to Talk To
and What to Say

Where to Begin?

Let's say for a moment that you're a freelancer in a field that serves a variety of businesses: a computer consultant. It's a Monday afternoon, you're in your office, you're a little nervous because business has been slow, and you're worrying about your bills, the economy, and your overhead. You're trying hard to find some new clients, but the beautifully designed and expensive mailer you just sent to the 2000 prospects on your mailing list resulted in a terrible response. You're thinking about chucking it all and moving to a fishing village in Mexico when you happen to pick up the business section of your local newspaper and see this:

> The Small Business Administration will be hosting its 15th annual awards banquet on April 10th at the Hyatt Plaza Hotel. Awards for achievement in small business management will be presented to Joan Darcy, CEO of Citywide Real Estate; Marilyn Hanks, president of Hanks & Company Advertising; Judith Golden, owner of Golden Glow health clubs; and Alfred Benjamin, president of Metropolis Record Company. Cocktails 6:00. Dinner 7:00. For reservations, contact Rosie Dworn at (213) 555-9999.

It's fairly clear from this listing that this event is going to appeal to small business owners in a wide range of industries, and most of them probably have computers. The recipients of the award represent everything from high finance to rap music, and after you've called for more information and learned that they're expecting 500 guests, you're convinced that somewhere in that room you just may find that new client you desperately need.

Here's another announcement that might appear in a publication you subscribe to:

> On October 5th the Southwest Museum will host a special screening of the new film *Five Black Stones*, which documents the journey of a Zuni Indian healer as he travels through the desert gathering herbs for a ceremony. A buffet supper will be served after the 7:30 p.m. screening. Tickets are $50, with proceeds going to the museum's Native American Cultural Fund. RSVP by Oct. 1st to Carole Lopez at (212) 555-1532.

At this event you'll be in the company of people who share your affinity for the Native American culture. The fact that they can afford the $50 admission price suggests that they are at least moderately affluent, and are likely to be involved in the world in a way that may be useful and interesting to you. It's possible that you just may find something you've been looking for here, whether it's a hot new business lead, the job you deserve, or someone to fall in love with.

These are two hot tickets. Let's go check them out.

Your Arrival

Contrary to popular myths about how fashionable it is to be late, when an invitation to a luncheon hosted by a professional association, for example, says "Cocktails at 11:30, lunch at 12:00," you should always arrive as close to 11:30 as possible.

This time has been designated specifically for socializing,

and it's usually the most productive hour of the entire day or evening because it's the only time to really do some serious mingling. It's prime time for talking to as many people as possible, because once lunch is served, you'll be confined to a table of six or eight people until it's time to go home. If you *are* lucky enough to find someone at your table who turns out to be a good contact, you'll barely be able to talk with her because, before the plates are cleared away, the speaker comes to the podium and you'll have to be quiet. So always arrive early, or at least on time.

Another advantage to early arrival is that you'll have a chance to meet the hosts before they get too busy, and they'll have some time to introduce you to the other early birds. By the time the room gets crowded, you'll have met at least two or three people, and you'll be chatting happily as if you knew everyone in the place.

The first few minutes we spend in a room are always the most awkward. It feels as though all eyes are turned toward us as we walk through the door and look around nervously while we try to determine what to do next. At many events, we're saved by the presence of a registration or sign-in table of some kind, which gives us something to do while we get our bearings. If at all possible, take your time in this area. Pick up any brochures or other materials that are displayed, and look through them briefly. You can use them as props later on. If you can position yourself so that you're not in the way but still have a clear view, say hello to other new arrivals as they check in. To them, you'll look as if you're part of the event, and since they too just arrived and aren't quite sure what to do, they'll see you as a good choice for their first conversation of the evening.

If you look around the room at the early stages of a gathering, you can see patterns in other people's behavior that mirror your own. New arrivals stand around for a minute trying to orient themselves to their surroundings. They may walk directly to the bar, and once they have a drink in their hands, turn around and face the room, surveying the action. Or they may simply continue a deep conversation with the person they brought along, shutting out the rest of the room until they feel secure enough to leave the cocoon. Some people might look around, lock eyes with someone, and march right over with a big hello, while others may quietly shrink into a corner and remain there all night. All these patterns are common, and no doubt you'll recognize yourself in at least one of them. It's comforting to know that no matter which style best describes you, you'll blend right in with everyone else.

Working the Room

At business functions, as well as at private parties, aggressive networking is not only accepted, it is encouraged, and it isn't viewed as being overly forward to approach strangers and introduce yourself. It's also considered perfectly acceptable to move in on a group and join their conversation. This is the preferred mode of behavior at most parties, and nobody will think ill of you for cruising through the room talking to as many people as you can and collecting business cards from those who interest you. Remember that other professionals are doing it too. Your actions won't be construed as rude or overly confrontive in any way.

You can work a room by being either mobile (circle the room talking to people and breaking in on groups) or stationary (position yourself in a strategic location, like the bar or buffet table, and hold court from there). A note of caution about the bar—drink moderately. Try watering down your wine or cocktail, or drinking nonalcoholic beverages. You'll do much better with all your senses intact than if you're even slightly inebriated. And never smoke in a room full of nonsmokers if you want people to talk to you!

Think of yourself as a *participant* rather than a guest. Parties are group activities, and you're on equal ground with everybody else in the room, so make it *your* party. It's a long-standing tradition in America for guests, when they arrive at a party in someone's home, to ask the host if he or she needs any help with the food or other tasks. It's mostly women who do this (though men should be doing it too), and it serves a very important purpose for the guests: It gives them *something to do*. If you find it difficult to start talking to people immediately, try getting involved in the preparations going on in the room. At a private party you can offer to help in the kitchen, greet guests, organize games or activities, clean up, or be in charge of the CD player. At a business party or charitable event, you might volunteer to distribute brochures, sell raffle tickets, or sign in arriving guests.

Who Can I Turn To? Easy versus Difficult Targets

Look around the room and try to get a sense of the people there. Who looks easy to approach? Who looks intimidating? Who looks confident and in control? What are they doing? Does someone look nervous or lost? Check out the people who're standing alone. They're always the easiest to talk to, because chances are good that they're feeling exactly like you are, having just arrived and not knowing a soul. They'll welcome you gratefully when you walk up and say hello. It's a scary prospect, but it's a risk worth taking. Remember the second commandment of Power Schmoozing: *Take risks.*

Another easy target that virtually guarantees success is the event's organizer or host. Though your hosts may be a committee rather than a person, you'll recognize them as the ones who greeted you at the door and perhaps took your money or issued you a name tag. It's their job to make sure people are mingling and having a good time, so don't hesitate to introduce yourself to them. If you tell them that you're new to the group (the first commandment of Power Schmoozing: telling the truth), they'll usually take a personal interest in you, taking you by the hand to be introduced around the room. It's a great way to get started, and highly recommended for several reasons. You'll be treated as if you're somebody special. You'll be laying the foundation for a relationship with the host, which can be further developed later on. It's extremely unlikely that you'll be snubbed or brushed aside. And you can depend upon your host to make an effort to connect you with people who share your interests.

The evening's speaker or guest of honor is always a good choice for an introduction or a quick hello. She'll most likely be an expert in the field in which the organization is involved, so if you have an interest in the group or its work, you'll have something to talk to her about. People who book themselves as speakers are exhibitionists at heart, and love to talk about themselves and what they do. The fact that they're there indicates their willingness to share themselves, particularly if they're in a position of being more knowledgeable than everyone else about a particular subject. Your approach—and the questions you ask—can be a great boost to their egos. And *do* ask questions! Never be afraid to admit when you don't know something. Asking questions gives the other person an opportunity to show off a little bit, and makes her feel like you're truly interested in what she has to say.

Very famous, very attractive, or very wealthy people always top the list of intimidating types. You'll usually find these people surrounded by others like them, or by admirers and hangers-on. But just because they seem inaccessible doesn't mean you shouldn't try. In fact, that's all the more reason to march directly up to them and take a risk. In Chapter 5, I've outlined some proven methods for dealing with intimidation, along with some easy and amusing exercises you can do to build confidence. One such exercise involves taking the direct approach by going right up to the most attractive or most powerful-looking person in the room and simply telling the truth. Try something like this:

"Hello. My name is Tom Brown. I couldn't help but notice that you seem to know everybody here, and you look very involved. I'm really interested in learning more about this group and meeting some of the people here. Are you a member?"

Does that seem too bold for you? If it does, good! Then it's exactly what you need to try. I promise you won't be disappointed—unless of course the person you're approaching is a stuck-up, shut-down, arrogant, emotionally crippled, mean, nasty person.

An approach like this can have a very flattering effect on someone, and the approach can be very, very simple. You don't have to be witty, brilliant, or funny. You just have to be *real*. Being direct is the best way to get over the fear of approaching "scary" people. They're scary only because we're under the mistaken impression that they're somehow better than we are.

Being Brave—With a Sense of Humor

Most of us feel that when we're at a party surrounded by strangers, we're being watched and judged. We try to conform to the mode of behavior that seems to be the norm for the evening. We try to dress the same way, talk the same way, be politically correct, eat the right foods, admire the right paintings on the wall, and generally, try to *fit in*, which actually makes us quite invisible. What if instead, we worked this hard to *stand out*?

Just for fun, here are some stories about how some of the bravest among us have managed to break the ice by throwing caution to the wind, using their sense of humor, and taking risks.

I observed one very interesting approach at an intimate nightclub where people were seated at small tables of two to four, dining, chatting, and listening to acoustic music. During the breaks in the show, people would get up and mingle, table-hop, and say hello to friends. Yvonne, a strikingly beautiful woman of about 35, didn't know anyone there, but didn't let that stop her from being at ease enough to walk past a man who was eating an exotic-looking shrimp dish and casually making a comment about how good it looked. He offered her a taste. Now most of us would have declined that taste because we—women especially—have been taught that we're not supposed to be truthful about our interest in food (and some people are paranoid about germs). But Yvonne gleefully accepted the shrimp, ate it with enthusiasm, said thank you, and launched into an energetic conversation with him ("...so how do you like the music? Are you a friend of the owner?"). Yvonne broke the ridiculous old rule of etiquette that says "When people offer you something to eat or drink, decline politely the first time they ask. It's OK to accept if they ask a second time."

At another event—an awards dinner honoring artists and designers in the advertising industry—executive types sipped Chardonnay and munched hors d'oeuvres while they browsed through a large exhibit of the nominated entries. One of the exhibits displayed videocassette boxes being honored for their design achievement in the category of adult entertainment, and on these boxes were pictures of buxom young women in lingerie. My friend Donna, a 37-year-old single mother networking for both business and marriage prospects, positioned herself directly in front of the exhibit, facing the room, so that anyone admiring the display would have to admire her as well. Each time an interesting prospect showed up to look at the boxes, Donna would smile and joke, "That's me on that box. I posed for that."

Donna doesn't look anything like the women on the boxes, so it was obvious that she was kidding around. It made everyone laugh immediately, and of course they'd make some clever comment, and a conversation would begin.

Not everybody feels comfortable being this playful. It takes a certain attitude, a willingness to be irreverent, and a commitment to taking risks. But what have you really got to lose? If you look at the things Donna and Yvonne did, it's hard to see how their actions could have hurt or embarrassed them or anyone else. The only real risk was that they might have approached someone who had no sense of humor, who would just stare blankly at them and offer no response. But the potential payoff is that they also might have approached someone fabulous, and had a lot of fun in the process.

There are other offbeat and humorous things you can do to make an impression on strangers. One of my students took the idea of telling the truth to an interesting extreme when he suggested this for an opening line:

"Hi. Who are you and what can you do for me?"

A little brazen perhaps, but it works in Hollywood because everybody knows that's why people are there, and everyone's so jaded that it's become a big joke. How about something a little more charming and vulnerable, like:

"Hi. I'm Ralph. I don't know anyone here. I don't even know you. Who do you know?"

Or this simple, nonthreatening one:

"Hi. You look like somebody I should know. My name's Amanda."

And finally, a line guaranteed to get a laugh:

"Hi. I'm Richard. I'm unemployed. I'm not rich. And I don't know anybody in show business."

Research and Preparation

When you're planning to attend an event that will be populated primarily by people you don't know (and upon whom you wish to make a good impression), preparation is vitally important. If you're going to be mingling with stockbrokers, it helps to know about current trends in the stock market. If you're going to a party at a yacht club, see what you can learn about some of the issues facing boat owners, such as the rising cost of boat slips and insurance. If you'll be attending a meeting of the Direct Marketing Association, learn about the concerns that affect that industry, like the negative impact of junk mail on the environment. (Don't call it junk when you're with them, though. They call it "direct" mail.)

But it isn't absolutely necessary to be a walking encyclopedia of facts and statistics. An easier approach is to simply work up some interesting questions to ask. Conversationally, you can do just as well, if not better, by simply having an interest in the issues. People with knowledge in a particular area enjoy answering questions from interested participants, so don't hesitate to ask, "How is the direct marketing industry dealing with pressure from environmental groups about unsolicited mail filling up the landfills?" *Never be afraid to admit you don't know something*. It's far better than *pretending* you do, only to get caught at it later.

Good preparation is the key to making you capable of interesting conversation. And the best source for up-to-date information can be found in special-interest publications.

For every business, cultural interest, art form, or political affinity in America, there's a magazine or newsletter dedicated to it. To find these publications, go to your local library and look for a directory called *Bacon's Publicity Checker*, which lists over 17,000 magazines and journals indexed by categories that cover everything from international finance to quilt making. You'll get quite a kick out of titles like *Flute Talk, The Fish Sniffer, Spudman* (for potato farmers—not a superhero), *Taxi News, Utopian Psychology,* and *Nude & Natural*. You can even get more specific if you're looking for a local angle, with publications like *Arizona Pharmacist, Cincinnati Bride,* and *Michigan Dry Bean Digest*. Of course, you'll also find the old standards like *Sports Illustrated, Variety, Architectural Digest,* and *Business Week*.

Reading special-interest publications gives you a quick fix on what's happening in any business, region, or mindset. Once you've identified the magazines you need, call and ask for a free sample copy, which they'll be happy to send (they know you'll have a hard time finding a copy of *Magnets in Your Future* at your local newsstand). Then start doing some serious reading. When you arrive at the party, you'll be ready to talk to anyone about the latest developments in ADD testing for children or the price of beachfront real estate in Malibu. For added effect, you can quote from the magazines you've been reading. ("I just read an editorial in *Tractor Times* about that very subject!") Go one better and carry a copy of the article with you as a conversation piece.

By the way, you should read your local paper and/or watch local and national TV news *every day*. Current events are always a worthwhile topic of conversation, and it's important to know what's going on in the world for the sake of your own well-being as well as for the sake of stimulating conversation. Read nonmainstream magazines and newspapers, such as the *Utne Reader* or the *Village Voice*, to get alternative views on hot issues.

Teamwork

Working as a team or going solo? Both approaches can be equally effective, and a lot depends on the groups you'll be mingling with.

When I was single, I preferred going alone to parties, bars, and other places where I might meet eligible men. I always thought young women looked insecure and silly traveling in packs, and I believed that I projected a more sophisticated image as a loner. It made me look deep, independent, and strong. In addition to that, cruising with a friend put limitations on me in terms of how long I wanted to stay somewhere, or where I might want to go afterward. Or with whom.

In the business world these considerations don't usually apply. In fact, teamwork can be a real advantage with the right partner. When my husband and I go to a business function—a lunch meeting of the International Teleproduction Society, for example—we go with the goal of schmoozing with as many people as possible. We arrive early (in time to take full advantage of the networking hour), and promptly split up. He goes one way, I go the other, and one by one, we single out individuals who look like they may have something to offer. We figure we've spent $50 to attend this function, and we have 1 hour in which to find the best prospects in the room. *That's why we're there.* Not for the food. Not for the ambience. And not necessarily to hear the speaker. But to make new friends and contacts. Period. If one of us meets someone whom we feel might interest the other, we take the prospect across the room for an introduction. Sometimes we'll choose separate strategic positions—one of us standing or sitting near the entrance, and the other circulating around the room. By the time the cocktail hour is over and everyone's being led into the other room for lunch or for the presentation, we've chosen the people we want to get to know better, and make a point of sitting with them. By then, we're ready to sit down with people we've prescreened, and can spend the rest of the time really getting to know them.

Business Cards and Other Accessories

One of the questions I am asked most often is "How and when do you give your business card to someone?"

Many people find this transaction awkward, even though they know that handing out a card in a business environment is as acceptable as using sunscreen at the beach. Yet the question remains: "When is the right moment?"

I've met people who have the unnerving habit of handing me their cards the moment they're introduced, way before it's even determined whether I'll ever have any reason to call them. It's a conditioned reflex, I suppose, for someone who's probably accustomed to making dozens of sales calls each day. I find it rather intrusive, especially when the card pusher turns out to be someone who doesn't particularly interest me.

It makes much more sense to check prospects out a little bit before you invite them to call you by giving them your card. If you bulldoze someone with your card before the two of you have exchanged 10 words, you may find a little further into the conversation that you've latched onto someone you can't bear, and you'll wish that you hadn't made yourself so accessible. Then what do you do when he starts calling you?

As you move through the room meeting new people, spend a few minutes talking to each one, finding out who they are, and how you might be able to include them in your life. If someone looks promising, by all means give him or her your card as soon as you've hit on a common thread (no matter what that thread may be):

HIM: ...so now my wife and I are trying to adopt a baby.

YOU: Really? Our 4-year-old is adopted! Before we found him, we went to a great adoption support group that really helped us. If you're interested, I have the number at my office. Why don't you give me a call on Monday, and I'll give you the number? Here's my card.

What a great way to make friends! In the business world, sometimes you'll be lucky enough to get someone who practically invites you to pitch them, and when that happens, don't hesitate. Remember, in a business environment, making connections for doing business in the future is the reason you're there. Everybody in the room knows it, so it's not the least bit inappropriate to do this:

HER: ...My book is going to be published in April, and I'm looking for a PR firm to organize a media tour for me.

YOU: Really? Well it just happens that I'm a PR consultant, and I've done several campaigns for self-help books like yours. I'd love to talk to you more about ways in which we might be able to work together.

HER: That would be great!

YOU: Why don't I call you later this week? Have you got a card? (Always get the other person's card or phone number! Don't simply hand out your cards and expect people to call you. The responsibility to follow up is yours.)

While business cards are certainly a must—they sure beat scribbling your phone number on the back of a matchbook—you can also be more creative about what you carry with you when you work a room. A business card is great for giving basic information like your name, number, and the name of your company, and maybe this information alone is enough to describe who you are and what you do. But often it's not sufficient. On Monday morning, when the 50 people you gave your card to at the weekend trade show get back to their offices and look over the 100 cards they've collected, what will your card tell them about you? How will they tell you apart from the other salespeople who pitched them all weekend?

For many productive people, one business card is not enough to inform the world about all their various endeavors. You can carry more than one card; one for your day job at a big accounting firm, and one for your sideline as a freelance tax preparer. This way, if you meet a prospective client for the firm, you give him the corporate card. If you meet the owner of a small hair salon who can't afford such sophisticated services, you can offer yourself as an affordable alternative.

For busy entrepreneurs and creative people involved in several projects at once, there's a way to take this concept one step further. I tell my students that part of arriving prepared at an event is to come armed with all the propaganda you've got—and then some. For some people, the answer to the question "What do you do?" can take 10 minutes to deliver, so you may have to be ready to present several different views of yourself, depending on who asks.

As an example, I never leave home without brochures for my PR consulting business. But if I meet someone who doesn't need PR services, who instead engages me in a stimulating conversation about separation of church and state, I'll be prepared to give him some information about a secular humanist group in which I'm involved. Conducting the Power Schmoozing seminars is a big part of my life, so I always carry flyers announcing upcoming seminars. I also carry flyers about a writer's workshop I conduct, and a few copies of each of my books are always in the trunk of my car.

That's an armful. But it can all fit nicely into a fashionable shoulder bag, and it's not as overbearing as it sounds. It's extremely important to be prepared, and professional people are impressed by good presentations. Seizing the moment by pulling out relevant sales information or service literature can help you leap-frog ahead of someone less prepared. Carrying printed information about yourself, your business, your services, the organizations you're involved with, and anything else you'd like to communicate, is a good way to guarantee you'll be remembered after the party's over.

How to Crash a Party

In the party culture of my youth, crashing a party was a bold, boisterous, and extremely cool thing to do. A group of uninvited teenagers in a car with deafening rock & roll on the stereo (preferably Led Zeppelin) would show up, and if they'd been lucky enough to score some beer or a few joints, they were welcomed inside. In the realm of civilized adulthood, the rules are exactly the same, but the game is played differently, with different props.

For adults—particularly in the business world—image is everything, so you can almost always walk right into a high-class private party simply by *looking the part*. At fancy affairs held in hotel ballrooms for instance, showing up in the proper attire and looking like you belong there will help you blend in with the crowd that's mingling over predinner cocktails. Once the doors are opened to the banquet room, a surge of people will start pushing through the doorway. All you have to do is walk right in with them, smiling at everyone, perhaps continuing a conversation that you'd started up moments earlier, and nobody will notice you.

If it's a very exclusive or very expensive party, and there are ticket-takers at the door making sure that only paid or invited guests make it through, you'll need to wait out the ticket-taking period. Head over to the hotel bar for a drink and return to the party area while dinner is in progress, or after it is finished. If the guards are still posted at the door (and usually by this time they've gone inside to join the others), then simply walk in as if you had been there all along, and are just returning from a visit to the bathroom or the phone booth. In most hotels, bathrooms and pay phones are located outside the ballroom area, and guests wishing to use them have to leave and return again. If you're properly dressed, and project an assured attitude, the odds are you'll go unnoticed.

This method for party crashing works most of the time. At the American Booksellers Association (ABA) convention each year, there are dozens of parties going on at any given time in one hotel or another, hosted by various publishers. Some are more private than others, but one year I crashed a very exclusive one—a glamorous party honoring a major publisher.

I happened to be at the hotel for another event, and was already wearing an evening dress. In the lobby, about 150 people were drinking and mingling, and there were ticket-takers at the door that led to the ballroom. Inside the ballroom I could catch glimpses of a big band playing swing music from the 1940s (my favorite), an open bar and buffet, and a room full of publishing bigwigs with whom I was desperate to schmooze. Nothing could stop me from getting into that room.

Since the preparty cocktail hour was taking place in a public lobby area, I bought a drink at the bar, planted myself in the middle of the crowd, and began talking to people. After a while, the crowd started moving toward the door of the ballroom, past the people checking names at the door. I waited until the crowd hit its fullest point, and then I simply placed myself along its outside edge, and moved into the room *with it,* making a point of talking to the person next to me as if he was my date. All I said to him was, "How are you doing? Looks like a great party." That was enough of a conversation to make me look as if I belonged there. The name-checkers didn't even notice me.

As professional New York party-crasher Richard Osterweil said in a recent *L.A. Times* article, "This is no game for the fainthearted. You need a lot of nerve." He told a story about the time he was using a fake Russian accent to impress Jackie Onassis at a New York gathering. The ploy worked beautifully until Mikhail Baryshnikov suddenly walked up and joined their conversation. In Osterweil's words, "I almost threw up."

So have fun, but use caution. It isn't necessary to go to extremes like using exotic accents, but some of Osterweil's party-crashing tips are well worth remembering:

- Dress as if you belong. Look rich. Nobody's going to refuse a rich person.
- To get past the gate, don't be aggressive. Be polite and confused. Or join a celebrity's entourage. There's so much attention focused on them, there'll be less on you.
- To get a table, find the maitre d' and say convincingly, "The people at our table are drunk and abusive. Can you find us another seat?"

A final note about party crashing: Avoid small parties full of people who know one another. Be sure it's a large enough group that no one will notice an outsider.

Social and Business Etiquette: Your Mother Was (Mostly) Right About These Things

In the business world, or in any world really, manners count. A lot. It's not difficult to get taken in by myths about how "hip" it is to forsake manners, especially in certain social circles where it's considered fashionable to be late, and cool to act indifferent, arrogant, or rude.

The *basic* rules of etiquette most of us grew up with still make sense if you're trying to make a good impression on someone, but there are, naturally, some exceptions. In certain situations, like a day-long pool party or an open house, it doesn't really matter much if you're late. Or in certain social niches —like partying with a heavy-metal rock & roll band—acting rude or being intoxicated just might be the preferred behavior.

So in situations that border on the ultra, use your instincts. And when in doubt, err on the side of politeness. But don't mistake wimpy, self-denying behavior for polite behavior. To listen attentively and maintain eye contact when someone is speaking is polite. To keep quiet when you're just burning to interrupt and make an important point is self-denial.

Following is an overview of some etiquette issues you might encounter in your daily life. The approach here is based, as usual, on truth telling, basic human ethics, and being yourself, as opposed to formality and tradition.

Lateness

It is rarely, if ever, acceptable to be late. Have you ever hosted a dinner party for eight friends, spent all day cooking a gourmet meal that you planned to serve at a certain time, and had half your guests show up 45 minutes late? *Without calling first?* That's truly uncaring behavior, and should certainly affect any future dinner invitations these people will receive.

There are three things you should never be late for: a business meeting, a romantic rendezvous, and lunch with your mother. In other words, you shouldn't be late for anything. It just isn't considerate to expect other people to put their lives on hold because of you, under any circumstances. If you must be late because you're stuck in a traffic jam or have an emergency business or personal issue that needs your attention, at least make the effort to call. But call as far in advance as you can. If your appointment is at 1:00, don't wait until 1:30 to call and say you're going to be late. I know people who are in the habit of doing this, and I have a very negative, *lasting* impression of them.

RSVPs

Always, *always* RSVP. No exceptions. No excuses. Do it right away, even if it's to say you're not sure yet. As a person who loves to throw parties and entertain, I'm constantly amazed at how often people just don't bother calling to say whether or not they'll be attending. Even at my own wedding, where guests were sent stamped, addressed reply cards, many of my friends didn't RSVP, and I had to call them at the last minute to get a head count for the caterer! Their responses ranged from, "Well, of *course* we're coming. We wouldn't miss your wedding for the world!" to "Gee, I'm really sorry. I misplaced the reply card and forgot all about it until just now."

That one was a real shocker, until I did some research and found out that many people don't bother to RSVP no matter *what* the occasion. It's terribly rude, and I'm amazed at how indifferent people can be about it. Hosts commit a lot of time and money to the parties they plan, and your RSVP is vital to their bottom line. When they request that you *respond, if you please,* they'll be very grateful when you do.

Sexism, Chivalry, and Respect

I love it when men open doors for me (and it doesn't happen often enough). And if you're a woman who spots a man with large packages approaching the door at the same time you are, you should most certainly open it for him (but ladies, be wary of this if you're in a deserted parking lot, dark alley, or empty building late at night).

Avoid language and attitude that may offend. In mixed company whose political, religious, ethnic, or sexual orientations you're unsure of, refrain from telling tasteless jokes or making tacky sexual innuendoes. Men, don't refer to your secretary as "my girl," or to a woman who is your peer in business as "the little gal in the marketing department." Avoid telling sexist jokes in the company of women (if you want them to like you), and *never* call a woman "honey" unless she's your wife, girlfriend, close friend, or daughter.

Please and Thank You

Thanks belong to everyone—your dinner partner when she refills your wine glass, the parking attendant, your office staff, your spouse, and your children. When my receptionist buzzes me on the intercom to tell me that Jane Smith is on line 2, I say, "Thank you." *Every time.* When my husband does the dinner dishes, I say thank you (*every month*). When my housekeeper does the laundry or cleans the bathroom—even though it's part of her job—I always thank her for doing specific jobs as she does them. When my children clean up their rooms, help carry packages in from the car, or do anything at all for me, I always say thank you. And guess what? They've learned how to do the same thing. When I'm eating breakfast with my 5-year-old, and he asks for more cereal, he automatically says, "Thanks, mommy" when I give it to him. Amazing but true.

Saying please and thank you is more than just polite. It demonstrates your respect for other people. It makes them feel good. And it increases their respect and desire to please and thank *you*.

Listen to Others While They're Speaking

If you're a guest at a networking-oriented event, it's acceptable to interrupt people who are talking casually in small groups in order to join the conversation. But in a one-to-one situation, you should generally try to let the person you're talking to finish what he or she is saying before you respond. Unless of course the person happens to be terribly boring and long-winded, and interrupting is the only way you'll be able to get a word in (or make your escape).

I once worked with a man in the advertising business named Dave, who had no conversational skills whatsoever. We worked on a project that required daily brainstorming sessions with two other people, and Dave usually spent our time ranting and raving about his wacko ideas while we'd listen helplessly for hours on end. As soon as one of us managed to take the floor for a minute, Dave's attention would start to drift. He'd shuffle through the papers on his desk, or involve himself in some other distraction, and within 15 seconds, he'd interrupt whatever the person was saying to begin bulldozing us with *his* ideas again, having never heard a word of the other person's contribution. Needless to say, Dave didn't have much luck in holding onto staff members or clients very long. They all had a chronic tendency to disappear on him.

Admittedly, Dave's an extreme example of a compulsive personality, but it never hurts to be on the lookout for similar tendencies in your own conversational style. The next time you're talking to someone, try waiting an extra *second* before you reply. Instead of formulating your answer, spend that extra second acknowledging what you've heard. The world begins to look a lot different when we stop trying to second-guess it, and just let it sing to us.

Look at the Person Who's Speaking to You

Eye contact is the most simple, basic rule of good communication, and the most difficult for most people to manage. You'll find that if you look into someone's eyes during a conversation, you will get—and be able to give—ten times more to that relationship.

It's rude to scope out the room over someone's shoulder while she's talking to you. It's understandable that at a certain point in a conversation you may want to start looking around for someone better to talk to, but try to be discreet about it, or better yet, try to end one conversation before you start looking for a new one. It's a common practice to keep one eye glued to the door in bars and at parties where everyone's looking for sexual opportunities, but it really makes the person on the receiving end feel like dirt. If you're not interested in the one you're talking to, simply excuse yourself and go somewhere else where you can get a better view of the action. Don't do it while he's offering his heart up to you.

Don't Be Physically Offensive

This is a rather sensitive area, so I'll get straight to the point. It's about having unpleasant body odors, wearing dirty clothing, or (for men) neglecting to trim ear and nose hair. For women, too much perfume or too much makeup can be a real turnoff.

Very tall people, men in particular, often use threatening body language without really meaning to, such as backing someone into a corner and hovering over them during a conversation. Some people have the annoying habit of standing too close when talking to someone they don't know well, or talking with a mouth full of food.

I once had dinner with a world-famous food critic who had the most atrocious table manners I had ever seen. He talked constantly and rapidly while shoveling food in his mouth at the same time. It was nauseating. This man has been wined and dined throughout the world by the most sophisticated of hosts, yet nobody—apparently not even his friends—had the nerve to tell him that his table manners left a lot to be desired.

These unconscious body behaviors can be very offensive, but you may never know whether you're one of the guilty ones. Will your best friend really volunteer to tell you if you have bad breath? Will a coworker take you aside and tell you that your perfume is unbearable? Maybe, but don't count on it. Instead, ask someone you love and trust—your spouse, your best friend, your mother, or even your kids—to give you a critique on the way you present yourself *physically*. Ask them to tell you about any annoying habits you may have, such as talking too loud, eating sloppily, interrupting others, telling tasteless jokes, having body odors, or using overly aggressive body language. This could be one of the most constructive conversations you've had in a long while, and may make a big difference in your life.

Don't Leave Brain-Dead Phone Messages

It's a high-tech, high-speed world out there, and there's no excuse for using up precious time and space inefficiently. Phone communication is extremely important, and leaving messages the wrong way can be a big time waster. Next time you leave a message for someone, give as much information as you can. For example, instead of saying, "This is Terri. Call me back at 555-0212," try something a little more informative, like: "This is Terri. Are you free for dinner on Tuesday? I'll be in your neighborhood around 6 o'clock." If the recipient returns your call only to get your voice mail, he can follow the same rule. Instead of saying, "Hi. I got your message. Call me back," he can make the communication easier by saying, "Tuesday's good for me. I've been wanting to try that new Thai restaurant on Riverside Drive. How's 6:30?" With that information, your plans can be confirmed with only one more call. You can have entire conversations this way, without ever talking face to face. It may sound cold, but it's the way things are.

In the business world, where millions of phone calls are made every day for the express purpose of asking and answering quick questions, think in terms of efficiency. When you leave a message with a receptionist or voice mail, state your question. The person you're calling can probably call you back with the answer, and, if you're not there, he can leave it on your voice mail. This way, the situation is handled with a minimum of missed calls. A more extensive version involves using the fax machine for messages. If your question or comment is long and involved, don't just leave a message with only your name and number and then wait for a call back. Send a fax with all the details. The person on the other end will then have all the information on paper, where she can see it, think about it, and formulate a response.

Be Cognizant of Cultural Differences

In our global culture as we approach the millennium, you'll be socializing more and more with people from a variety of ethnic groups, nationalities, religions, cultures, and belief systems. Make a point of learning what people from other cultures consider polite, because it may be very different from what you're used to.

A little research can reveal, for instance, that in a certain culture it's considered offensive to look directly into someone's eyes. In Middle Eastern countries, it is quite common and a sign of respect for men to touch each other, to greet one another with a kiss on each cheek or with a sincere, strong hug. In homophobic America, however, the same action might be perceived as an unwelcome sexual come-on.

On the other hand, while the Japanese have many taboos and restrictions on social behavior in their own country, it is generally accepted that in America, Japanese businesspeople expect Americans to act like Americans. Therefore, it is not considered offensive to be assertive about introducing yourself to a Japanese person at a cocktail party with a good old American handshake. In Japan, however, a completely different set of rules might exist.

Smoking cigarettes is an interesting example. It's a habit that is now taboo, or at the very least politically incorrect, in many American social circles. But in parts of Europe, you'll find that smoking is as popular as ever, and to ask someone to refrain from smoking in your presence would be extremely presumptuous. In another example, a woman breast-feeding her baby in public isn't even noticed in most of the world. In America, she can get arrested for it.

So before you cross cultural lines in your schmoozing efforts, check the rules. Do a little research about the norms in other countries and other cultures to make sure you're not offending anyone. Rules of etiquette exist for a reason—to ensure that people don't go around making one another feel uncomfortable, angry, or embarrassed. But there's latitude available in every social environment, so give yourself a moment to check out the etiquette standard at each event you attend, and then just go with the flow. If you smoke, but you're in a room with 100 other people and none of them are smoking, it would be best to refrain. If you're constantly showing up at parties on time but you're always the first to arrive and the hosts are still in the shower when you get there, you can conclude that lateness might be acceptable in this crowd.

Allow room for flexibility, but always respect the enduring rules that make sense, like remembering to RSVP and calling ahead if you're going to be late. This is the kind of behavior that makes you a good guest, and will always be remembered by the people who invite you over to play with them.

Finally, remember to be yourself and to have fun! If you're at a party where the behavior codes are so strict that you're a nervous wreck all night, then you're not going to enjoy yourself very much. Respect the rules of etiquette, of course, but don't hesitate to take risks and use your personality to break the ice when necessary. You'll find that your honesty and relaxed style will be a welcome relief to a lot of the people in the room who are working so hard to conform. If it isn't, it may be time for you to start socializing with a looser crowd.

*   *   *   *   *

Behaviors and Attitudes That Draw People In

1. A great sense of humor
2. Good manners
3. Confidence
4. Nonthreatening appearance
5. Smiling and eye contact
6. Starting a conversation instead of waiting for someone else to do it
7. Knowledge about the subjects at hand
8. Knowing when to let go
9. Not taking yourself too seriously
10. Fearlessness
11. Respect for cultural differences

*   *   *   *   *

*   *   *   *   *

Behaviors and Attitudes That Push People Away

1. Smoking (some exceptions)
2. Drunkenness
3. Sloppy appearance or bizarre fashion statements (acceptable in some circles)

4. Hostile or depressed disposition
5. Excessive profanity (also acceptable in some circles)
6. Bad jokes
7. Talking too much
8. Talking too little
9. Too much hype, jive, and name dropping
10. Bad manners
11. Offensive odors or body language

*   *   *   *   *

Overcoming Fear and Intimidation

Those of us who reached adulthood before the "me" generation gave us permission to love ourselves had some very strong notions ingrained in our thinking about how to behave in proper society. One of the strongest messages we received had to do with the "S" word. Selfishness. It was a big no-no.

When I was growing up in the 1950s, a plethora of non-negotiable golden rules dictated the way people should act. Looking back at those rules, it doesn't surprise me that most of the people who take my classes are fearful about stepping forward and asking to be noticed. Look again at the old rules in Chapter 2 and notice how absurd they sound.

Why We're Afraid to Ask for What We Want

In most of mainstream America, well-bred children were taught that it was terribly impolite to *ask* Aunt Agnes for a cookie while visiting at her house. It was considered more respectful to wait until the cookies were offered, and many times, even if we were *ravenous* for those cookies, it was considered more polite to decline. The message: It's not *nice* to ask for what you want. Selfishness was frowned upon by our parents, while self-effacing behavior was rewarded. This was particularly true for little girls, many of whom grew up to be the women who created a political movement in the 1970s just to claim their right to ask for what they want in the work-place, in the bedroom, and in life.

Many of us were taught as children that to honor our own needs, to try to mold the world into one which suits us, is somehow immoral, and that a world full of people with such selfish values would lead to social chaos and moral decline. So we learned to deny our self-worth, and worked hard to avoid being viewed as conceited, playing down any compliments that were given to us, not acting proud of our accomplishments, and above all, not asking for what we want.

Then one day we became adults, with grown-up jobs and needs that required us to break some of these rules in order to succeed. And what happened? We found ourselves socially and emotionally crippled, unable to ask for the recognition and support we deserve.

This is why the Power Schmoozing seminars attract intelligent, professional adults who are terrified of introducing themselves to strangers. What they all seem to have in common is the belief that taking an aggressive approach to socializing is impolite, irresponsible, egomaniacal, and socially taboo.

What they're left with is the "F" word. Fear.

The Three Fears

Think about exactly why walking into a room full of strangers and asking to be noticed is so frightening. You'll probably find that your fears fit into one or more of these groups.

1. Rejection

The most obvious is the fear that you're going to introduce yourself to someone who's going to hurt you by making an insulting comment, ignoring you rudely, or walking away. At the root of this fear is your notion that she's responding this way *because of you*—because you did something *wrong*.

We were taught as children that imposing our presence on

someone who did not specifically ask for it was rude. But this is just not true in the adult world. What *is* true is that many people out there are in a lot of pain about things that have nothing to do with you, and because of this, they can be rude, neurotic, hostile, shut-down, or stuck-up. So give yourself a break. If the person you've just introduced yourself to has an attitude problem, just move on to someone else. Because it's *her* problem. You're under no obligation to take on her negative energy and make it your own. And you're certainly not obliged to heal her or transform her.

2. Appearing Too Aggressive

The fear of being too aggresive begins with the mistaken idea that there's something tacky about working a room for personal gain. If you believe this, try looking at it another way.

Consider the high-powered, glitzy social events—like $1000-a-plate fund-raisers for charities or political causes—that occur in your city. People who can afford an evening like this put on their tuxedos and gowns and go to posh events *for one reason only*—because they want to network. Naturally they care about the charity, but if supporting the charity was their *only* intention, they could accomplish that by staying home and sending a check. Instead, they choose to go in person, because they want to see and be seen. They want to make contact with others. To mingle. To Power Schmooze.

Many of us think that when we attend an event like this we're supposed to put on a pretense about our reasons for being there. We're supposed to pretend that our motivations are 100 percent philanthropic—that we're thinking only about saving the rain forests or helping abused children, and not at all about bettering our own lives. (Remember the rule that says to always think of others before yourself?)

Why not be real about it? Acknowledge freely that attending these events is good for *you*—not just because it feels good to support the cause, but because it helps provide you with friends and an active social life. What's wrong with that?

Charity events provide the foundation for the glamorous

social lives of many important people, and attending is nothing to be embarrassed about. Nobody's going to call the behavior police to report you for acting like a hungry shark. People are there to meet one another, and to share information. Everybody agrees that it's acceptable to do this.

3. Being "Found Out"—The Impostor Syndrome

You've heard of this one. It's the fear that in the middle of your pitch to the most important big shot in the room, he's going to ask you a question that you can't answer, or put you on the spot to deliberately intimidate you, *and then he'll find out that you're not as smart or important or successful as you say you are.*

Has this really ever happened to you? Has someone ever just turned and run away from you in disgust after unmasking your outrageous pretense? Not very likely. And even if such a thing had begun to happen, honesty would have saved the day. Telling the truth is always the best way out of a tight corner. Employing a sense of humor along with it is even better. Remember the story about Carrie and Bill Gates.

Admittedly, there are times when a little masquerading can bring you some real results. So if you must stretch the truth a little when trying to impress someone, take on as little risk as possible. You can cover yourself by doing some research in advance, sticking to vagaries and basics, and smiling a lot. But even in this situation, don't hesitate to ask questions if you really don't know something (and you're sure it won't blow your cover to ask about it). Still, the best solution, and the one I recommend 100 percent of the time, is simply to tell the truth about who you really are. Admit your lack of knowledge when you don't know something. Don't be afraid to ask questions. Most often, it makes the person you're talking to feel like he's knowledgeable, and it's a good way to keep the conversation, not to mention the mutual respect, going.

Each of these three fears addresses at least one of our terrifying negative fantasies about the ways in which we might get hurt if we take a risk. But if you look back over your life, can you see how, in many situations, taking that risk launched you into another, more secure level where you operated more effectively? Living proof that *taking risks* doesn't mean you can always expect to get hurt. In fact, the times when you do get hurt often herald an important step along the path to some magnificent change that was due to happen in your life anyway.

Here's a little story about a frighteningly embarrassing moment that I experienced, which addresses these fears perfectly. This makes the top of the Ten-Most-Embarrassing-Things-That-Can-Happen-During-a-Cocktail-Party list, but you'll see how honesty and a sense of humor helped save the day.

I was attending a groundbreaking party for an important client of mine, an architect. It was a fancy affair, full of politicians and real estate developers in tuxedos, milling around a decorative shallow pool in the new building's courtyard.

It was very crowded, and I was trying to make my way around a knot of people standing at one corner of the pool. Instead of being bold enough to say, "Pardon me," and asking them to make room so I could pass, I decided that, rather than *bothering them,* I would try to step across the corner of the pool. Well, of course I slipped, and in I went. Fortunately the pool was only about 12 inches deep, so I didn't go under. I just landed there with my rear end in the water and my legs sticking out in a most unflattering manner.

Everyone rushed to my aid—powerful, wealthy men and women, the *mayor,* and of course my client. It was incredibly humiliating as they picked me up and tried to help me regain my dignity. I was sure they all thought I was drunk (I wasn't), and that my client would fire me the next day for embarrassing him in front of *his* clients (he didn't).

I looked around at the horrified faces staring at me, and out of some kind of survival instinct, my sense of humor kicked in, and I said, "Would the person I'm supposed to sue please step forward?" Everyone laughed nervously with relief, and after assuring them that I was OK, and only kidding about a lawsuit, I accepted a drink kindly handed to me by a sympathetic real estate broker. He sat with me while I composed myself, and in a few minutes we were talking business. He turned out to be a potential client, but that's not the point of the story.

Throughout the rest of that evening, every time other guests saw me, they'd ask if I was all right. I ended up having conversations with interesting people whom I probably would not have met if I hadn't fallen into the pool. My instinctive, easygoing attitude turned my "disaster" into a great networking tool, and it turned out to be a wonderful evening—where I was the star.

Of course you don't have to be a comedian who comes prepared with clever comeback lines for every faux pas that occurs. It's really just a matter of *not taking yourself too seriously.* If you don't think of yourself as a fool, neither will anybody else. By having a light—as opposed to heavy—attitude, you can control the way things turn out. When you allow yourself to see that everyone in the room is just as vulnerable as you are, that they are just as likely to fall into the pool as you are, the world starts to look not just different, but a whole lot better.

In my seminars we do an exercise that helps us get a better sense of how we're all equals in the fear department (I learned this exercise in a wonderful workshop entitled Making Love Work, conducted by Barbara de Angelis).

In a room of 30 or more people, I ask everybody to look around and silently select someone who looks appealing, safe, and easy to approach. Once their selections are made, I ask them to look around again, but this time, to find someone who looks intimidating—someone they'd normally hesitate to approach. Once these selections have been made, I surprise them all by asking them to get up from their seats, and go introduce themselves to the person they've chosen as intimidating—*and to tell the person why he or she was chosen!*

At this point, a ripple of terror starts spreading through the room, but one by one, people get up and start doing the exercise. Soon the room is filled with astonished pairs of people engaging in what may be one of the most candid conversations of their lives, and after 15 minutes of this I have to practically pry them apart with a crowbar.

After the exercise, I invite those who are so inclined to stand up and tell the rest of the group about their experience. What they find time and again is that the person they picked as intimidating turned out to be not the least bit scary. Maybe it was someone in a similar business, or someone going through a divorce, or someone with a severe shyness problem. A 30-something starving artist might choose a well-dressed older man because he looks successful and reminds him of his father, a wealthy conservative banker who doesn't approve of his son's lifestyle. But then it turns out that the chosen man is a retired dentist who's taking jazz piano lessons and lives on a houseboat. Or a young secretary might view a 55-year-old woman dressed in sedate business attire as an uptight authority figure. But isn't the secretary surprised when she finds out that the woman is a sex therapist! I'm serious. This really happens.

You really can't judge people by their outward appearances. And the rewards for taking a risk and making an attempt to scratch the surface of strangers are enormous. You learn that you have as much right to be in that room as they do, and that no matter how many troubles you're having in your life, how much fear, how much expectation of being hurt, someone else is probably having *more*.

I learned this by way of a little experiment I conducted several years ago when I was waiting for a friend on a street corner in a small town. I was bored, and I was sitting in my usual manner, eyes downcast and arms folded across my chest, and keeping myself tucked securely into my own little bubble. Out of boredom perhaps, I decided to amuse myself by trying to make eye contact with the people passing by. I'd try to catch the eye of each person who walked past me, just long enough to connect and flash a little smile. I had no idea this little exercise would be so powerful, and that it would transform my life.

The people walking by were locked into their little bubbles too—until my stare woke them up and pulled them out. I'd beam each one of them a huge smile, with direct eye contact and a nonthreatening "Hello," and most of them did double-takes, surprised by the intrusion. But *all* of them, after recovering from the shock of being unexpectedly ejected from their armor, responded with such warmth, such relief at having been contacted, that I realized how *isolated* most of us are during a typical day. Each person I connected with in this way would light up when he or she caught my smile, smile back and say hello, and then begin to shut down again after passing me. It was a real revelation to realize how desperate and how willing we are to break out of our cocoons and connect with one other. All we seem to need is *permission*.

From that day forward I knew that I had the power not only to pull *myself* out of isolation, but to pull others out as well. Perhaps if I'd been standing on some mean street in the inner city smiling at people, I'd have gotten into trouble. But it never occurred to me for a moment that someone would get angry at me, hurt me, or criticize me for sitting there communicating in such a pure and simple way. It was a risk worth taking.

It takes just as much energy to dream up a negative fantasy as a positive one. We humans have this propensity for bringing our sense of unworthiness with us wherever we go, with all our expectations that we're not good enough, and it can have a debilitating effect on our lives. Asking for someone's attention and then doing something interesting with it can be very scary. But remember, *everyone else is just as afraid as you are.*

If you don't believe this, just look around you. Try standing on the street someday smiling at people. Then try some of the following exercises designed to help you practice Power Schmoozing in your daily life. I guarantee that if you practice these behaviors for 6 months, your personality—and your entire universe—is going to change dramatically.

Everyday Dress Rehearsals

If you have trouble starting a conversation with a stranger, or if you feel that wherever you go you're all alone and nobody wants to talk to you, here are some exercises that may help you feel more confident. You can do these anywhere, any time, with little or no risk.

1. Talk to People in Elevators

Have you ever noticed how everyone stands silently in an elevator, staring straight ahead? There appears to be an unwritten rule that tells us not to speak to one another in elevators. Who made up such a rule? Is it part of the building code?

Elevators offer the perfect opportunity to engage someone for a quick hello. Simply make eye contact, smile, and say, "Hi." Or, "What a gorgeous day." Or, "What a slow elevator." Anything will work. This is a low-to-no-risk activity. And you can do it with confidence, knowing that you're going to be there for only a minute, and you'll probably never see the person again. The idea here is to simply practice talking to strangers, not to make a business contact or a lifelong friend, necessarily (although that can certainly happen).

For the very bold, next time you enter an elevator, try this icebreaker. Instead of walking in and immediately turning your back on everybody, do the opposite. Walk in, and don't turn around. Keep your back to the door *and face the other people.* They'll look at you like you're crazy, but you can smile and say, "I'm taking a course in how to overcome shyness, and one of our assignments is to do this in an elevator." I guarantee you'll get a laugh, and you'll leave that elevator feeling great about yourself.

2. Practice Longer Conversations

Beginning today, start talking to people in bank lines or grocery store lines. In the checkout line, point to the latest trash on the front page of the tabloids and say "I saw Elvis; just the other day at the laundromat." Sometimes all you have to do is just say, "Hi." You probably won't find someone to love or your dream job by doing this, but you will get used to the idea of connecting with strangers.

Practicing on strangers is a great way to become a better and more spontaneous conversationalist. And this exercise is easy, because you know you're going to be with this person for only a few minutes. The encounter will probably be over before you run out of things to say. Unless, that is, you find some real interest between you.

3. Talk to Less Intimidating People

Practice on the UPS driver, the mail carrier, the receptionist at the office you're calling, the waiter at the catered event, or your auto mechanic. These people are obliged to be polite, but are available for more interesting conversation. They are also just as important as anyone else in your world, and can become valuable allies.

4. Be Really Brave—Try the Direct Approach

Why not single out an intimidating person, walk right up to him, and say, "I've been wanting to talk to you, but I've been afraid to approach you." This speaks so directly to people's egos that they find it irresistible to ask you why. Not only has a conversation begun, but it's a very efficient one, cutting right through the B.S.

5. Practice Taking Risks

Go to a gallery opening and congratulate the artist. In the business world, when you hear about someone doing something that interests you, pick up the phone and call him (you can get a lot of leads by reading the trade publications). Go to a lecture on a subject you're familiar with and introduce yourself to the speaker. Approaching powerful people with admiration for their work flings open the doors of opportunity.

6. Have Fun!

Contrary to what your parents or your church may have taught you when you were little, life *is* fun. None of this is supposed to be deadly serious. We're here to expand ourselves, to think freely, and to love. And those processes can be a lot of fun.

The payoff for taking these risks is that if you're aggressive about bringing new people into your universe, your universe is going to expand. Which means it will continue to fill up with a cornucopia of new ideas, new friends, and new opportunities that wouldn't have been there if you hadn't opened your mouth and said hello to someone. So don't be afraid to use your powers of communication.

You're not alone out there.

CHAPTER

SIX

The Psychology of Schmoozing

The only awkward moments that occur in the Power Schmoozing seminars are the ones in which a student—usually one who's struggling with a deep-rooted emotional issue that prevents him from taking charge of his life—persists in asking questions about how to overcome his personal psychic hurdles. Many times, a student will make a statement like, "I really do want to be better at talking to people at parties, but my wife always does all the talking, and never lets me get a word in."

When I hear comments like these, my temptation is to launch into my stock self-empowerment speech, in which I point out to the poor guy that he's in an unhealthy addictive relationship with his wife, that he actually does have a choice about his behavior *and* his life, and that he's living in fear, married to someone just like his mother who probably abused him as a child, blah blah blah. That's my temptation. But I don't do it. I just let it be, because it's not my job to fix him. It's not why he signed up for the seminar, and I don't want to make it my job to rip his armor off in one fell swoop. There's probably another seminar going on down the hall that will do that for him.

Being a Victim

One evening, a woman in the class—I'll call her Lucy, a secretary at a major film studio—persisted in interrupting my lecture every few minutes to engage me in this dialogue:

ME: ...so those are three good ways to break the ice.

LUCY: (*raising her hand*) Excuse me, but I go to a lot of parties with people in my business, and they're all very rude and won't let anybody talk to them.

ME: OK, that can be a legitimate problem. Let's talk about what to do when you're dealing with a stuck-up crowd. (*I proceed to give the class some techniques for dealing with arrogant behavior*)

LUCY: (*in response to my suggestion that a good technique is to engage people in small talk about current events in the world*) But they aren't interested in the world. They're interested only in themselves.

ME: OK. Then encourage them to talk about themselves! People are flattered by that. Self-centered types love an audience. Here are some ways you can lead the conversation in that direction...

LUCY: (*whining*) But it's impossible to even *start* a conversation with them. They won't even say hello to anyone.

ME: (*the rest of the class is beginning to sigh and shift around uncomfortably*) These people are in the film industry, you say? Can't you talk to them about current films? Read *Variety* the day of the party, and get yourself up to speed on how much money was raked in by the movies that opened the previous weekend...

LUCY: (*really distressed*) You don't understand. These people don't care about the film business. There's nothing you can talk to them about. They're horrible people...

By now, the other students are getting impatient and feeling embarrassed for poor Lucy. They begin trying to get us all out of this ridiculous impasse by contributing their comments.

"What are they—all zombies?" someone says to Lucy, who nods her head in the affirmative.

"You don't really believe that these bigwigs don't know or care anything about their own business, do you?" asks someone else defiantly.

"If you hate them so much, maybe you should be in another business," suggests another.

Power Schmoozing is a self-improvement activity. By its very nature, it touches the deep personal hang-ups people have about shyness, insecurity, fear of rejection, sexuality, abandonment, and other hot issues. It more than touches them—it barrels down on them like a Mack truck.

In class that night, it was obvious to everyone that Lucy's problem was *her*, not the people in her industry. She was insecure, unhealthy looking, poorly dressed, and—as I discovered later when she cornered me after class to complain more about how impossible life was for her—a truly lost soul. She called herself a filmmaker, but admitted that she had never made a film. In fact, she'd never attended film school, or even a local college extension course on the subject. When I asked if she was working on a script or an idea for a movie, she said no, she hadn't gotten to that point yet. And she had a hundred reasons.

Lucy's victim mentality is classic. She was controlled by fear and self-doubt, and felt so powerless to shift that position that she lived her life at the mercy of everyone—and everything—else. And it was a big, mean world out there for her. Lucy didn't have the skills to harness power for herself, and she hadn't taken any steps to learn those skills. Sadly, it usually takes a big shock or a lot of emotional pain to drive us into therapy, recovery, or self-help programs, and only then do we wake up and realize that we can take control of our lives. It was easier for Lucy to decide that the evils of Hollywood were stopping her from getting a life. Easier to blame something, or someone else. It wasn't much different from the man who said that his wife never let him speak. It took all the tact I could muster to keep from telling him to get a new wife. But that's exactly the statement I wanted to make. Own your life. Change what doesn't work.

On the surface, Power Schmoozing appears to be about going to parties and dazzling people with your conversational skills. But that dazzle is just a by-product. When you scratch the surface you see that it's really about believing that you can go into the world and make it work for you. It's not about just sitting back and taking whatever comes down the pike and calling it your life. Each new day is an opportunity to *make your life,* to create your reality. Because if you don't, you're just going to get table scraps while it looks like everyone else is getting a gourmet meal. Just ask Lucy.

You can never separate any aspect of your life—your business, your love life, or your family relations—from the condition of your own psyche. If you believe, as I do, that the world is basically a blank screen ready to receive your projections, then you can start changing your reality today. The opposite side of that belief is to think that you're helpless, with no control over what happens to you.

This has been a hotly debated philosophical and religious question for centuries: Do we or don't we have a say in what happens to us? Without getting too cosmic or esoteric, I believe that some experiences are indeed random, like falling off a horse and breaking your leg, or winning the lottery. But there is a point at which you have control, and that point comes *when you make a decision about that experience.* When you say, "I fell off a horse and it was so terrible that I'll never ride again," *that's* a decision. And that's the kind of decision that *creates your future.*

How many of us have made choices like this about romantic relationships? Most of the time our decisions are made subconsciously, so they're harder to recognize. But they're in there, alive and kicking in our minds, and they dictate the way we live every day, at least until we realize we can change them.

Psychology tells us that we gravitate toward the familiar because we're driven and at the same time protected by an ego which only wants to be *right.* So if we were abandoned by a parent as a child, in our adult life we'll try to duplicate that feeling, only because we know it so well. It can take years of psychotherapy to recognize these patterns. Isn't it interesting how we're more willing to feel uncomfortable and isolated than we are to feel safe and at ease?

The idea of acting with great confidence frightens and embarrasses us. And we consider timid, self-effacing behavior to be polite. We have a notion that a person who's acting bold, who's drawing attention to herself and asking for recognition, is on an "ego trip." But the big surprise is that *you actually have to drop your ego in order to act that way.* It's our obsession with ourselves and how imperfect we feel we are that keeps us from truly being comfortable in our bodies and in the world.

If you're really ready to start taking charge of your life and going after the things you want, congratulations. You've arrived at a deliciously terrifying and exhilarating turning point. Don't cop out now. If it's going to work, you have to go all the way. If you smoke, and it's a turnoff to the person or the crowd you want to hang out with, then quit. If you're overweight and it presents a social obstacle for you, get into a diet program and lose the weight. And if you're in a marriage that doesn't work, if your spouse gets jealous every time you say hello to another human being, or doesn't support you in your goals and dreams, then you might want to consider counseling, or getting out of that relationship.

Overcome your addictions. Lose weight. Quit that job you hate and make a commitment to finding a better one. Get out of an abusive relationship. Give away everything you own and move to an uncharted tropical island if that's what you've always dreamed of. If you're taking better care of other people than you are of yourself, then get into therapy and find out why. Be willing to change, even if it may hurt or displace someone who has an investment in keeping you the same.

Communicate. *Take a risk. Tell the truth. Break the rules.* That's how to own your life.

How to Start Healing Yourself

One of the great contributions my generation made to our culture was the development of self-help programs: books, classes, therapies, seminars, and a thousand other channels through which to rid ourselves of negative emotional baggage. For some people, shyness is the only thing that stands between them and the rest of the world, and the solution can be as simple as taking an acting class or a seminar on overcoming shyness. For others it might be more serious, such as dealing with the emotional scars of childhood sexual abuse. The common denominator is that every one of us is carrying some kind of "stuff" around that stands in our way. The good news is that we now have access to tools that can help us get beyond those obstacles.

A friend of mine named Eddie who is a brilliantly talented musician became homeless last year at the age of 40 because he wouldn't take a menial day job to survive. His parents were obsessive overachievers, and all his life he was under pressure to compete with his father, a rich and successful musician. When Eddie landed in Los Angeles in his late thirties and tried to make it in the music business, the entire music scene became an extension of his childhood pressure cooker, and he simply refused to compete. So even though Eddie never stopped talking about how his plan was to become a successful recording artist with a deal on a major label, he spent his days playing guitar for spare change on the beach, wore tattered clothes, and had a bitter, negative attitude, which made him not too pleasant to be around. Eventually he could no longer pay his rent, and ended up living in his car.

Eddie had the tools to attain what he said he wanted—talent, intelligence, and friends who were willing to help him—but he pushed them all away. His unexpressed anger and his feelings of unworthiness were so intense that they turned inward, and drove him to the opposite extreme.

There are a million stories like Eddie's in the big city, not to mention small towns and villages throughout the world. But there are also a million opportunities to *change your story.* Start by looking deeper into yourself. Be brave. It can hurt, and it can feel very threatening, because everything that has become familiar and comfortable to you is subject to change. The more you work on it, the faster the changes come, so hold on to your hat. Here are some activities that are guaranteed to help.

1. *Take stock of gains and losses.*   Make a list of what you would gain by becoming successful in your endeavors. And then make another list of what you would *lose* by becoming successful. Notice how some of the things you might lose include some things *you need to lose,* such as a marriage that causes you more pain than joy, or the approval of your

parents, which has nothing to do with your approval of yourself.

2. *Take classes and attend seminars.*   Local newspapers list classes, seminars, and lectures on many subjects, from starting a business to recovering from divorce. You have nothing to lose by attending, and everything to gain. (At the very least you'll meet people with similar interests. And remember, they're just as unsure of themselves as you are.)

3. *Reveal yourself and your feelings to your friends.*   Your friends understand your psyche better than you think they do. Open up and let them help. Tell them what you're struggling with; talk about your dreams, but also your fears. Friends who really want you to be happy are the greatest support system of all, so don't shut them out when you need them most just because you're trying to be strong. They don't want you to be strong. They want you to be you.

4. *Get professional help.*   It's unfortunate that psychotherapy has had such a bad image in our culture for so many years. Now, thankfully, it's finally becoming more acceptable, but it's still considered "weird" in traditional pockets of society. Why is it normal to go to a mechanic to fix your car, a teacher to help you learn, a doctor to heal your body, but not a therapist to help heal your heart?

   It isn't hard to find a good therapist or counseling group. Just ask your friends. Everybody knows one. Also, self-improvement seminars are remarkable tools for personal change. At the very least, being in a room full of other people who are trying to feel better about themselves makes you feel like you're not the only one struggling. And that can be a great load off your mind.

5. *Stop associating with people who don't support you emotionally.*   If your parents constantly tell you that you'll never amount to anything, then stop talking to them. If someone in your life is trying to control or manipulate you, disconnect from that person. If you have "friends" who take advantage of you, then it's time to cut them loose.

   Take the risk that you might be alone for a short time,

knowing that soon, you'll find new and better friends, simply because you took charge of your life. If anything is standing in the way of your being emotionally healthy and in control of your own life, then get rid of it. And that means addictions too—drugs, alcohol, cigarettes, or food.

6. *Take action.* When you hear about an activity or program that might help get you to the next step toward your goals, do it! If a friend invites you to join her at a lecture on healing unhealthy relationships, go, no matter how painful the confrontation may be for you. Your friend will be there to help you.

Sounds like quite a list of work, doesn't it? It is. And none of it is easy. In fact, it's the hardest work you'll ever do. But what's wonderful about it is that you get the best payback in the world when you do it. You get to stop being in pain. You get to stop being alone.

None of it happens instantly. It takes a lot of work and a lot of time and a real commitment to changing your life. And you can't do it alone. You need your friends and your family (if they're supportive of the changes you're trying to make) to encourage you and love you. There's a whole world of possibilities waiting for you out there.

What does all this have to do with Power Schmoozing? Maybe nothing for some people. Maybe everything for others. It's a matter of working on the whole picture—not just the social skills, which are really on the surface, but on the things that really drive you, and the ways in which you might be blocking your own success.

It's like the story of Lucy. I wanted to tell her that she was projecting her own sense of isolation onto the people in her world. She saw these people as empty shells with nothing to say, yet they were all active, successful, creative people with busy lives and tons of energy. Lucy was out of touch with a source of similar strength in herself from which to approach them. But these inner sources can be developed with a little work and a little help. You just have to start by believing that it's possible, and that you are entitled to them.

The Dating Game—
Without the Games!

Could any of us born before 1965 have imagined that the day would come when we could stop playing silly little games with one another in the dating world? When I was growing up in the 1950s and early 1960s, conventional wisdom held that in order to be considered "nice girls," there were two things we must never do:

1. Have sex of any kind
2. Exhibit assertive behavior of any kind

Meanwhile, the boys were told something quite different:

1. Have sex with as many tramps as you can, but marry a *nice* girl
2. Be in control of all things at all times

From the beginning of time until the 1970s, women have understood that their lot in life was to suffer in silence while boys and men heaped an abundance of indignities upon them. It was a wise and saintly woman who could sweetly and understandingly forgive a man for minor infractions such as not calling when he said he would (after waiting for days by the phone), forgetting anniversaries or birthdays (a bouquet of flowers a few days later made things all better), or having extramarital affairs (a midlife crisis, probably her fault for gaining weight after the kids were born). It was considered unladylike and unwise for a woman to demand respect and attention—that would be nagging, and men *hate* that. And of course we would never show jealousy, because it was very unbecoming, even though it was flattering to see men get jealous over us (it was often the only way we could be reassured of our value to them).

We women were at our most heroic when we succeeded at keeping quiet and refraining from lodging complaints about not being treated fairly, no matter how much rage and anger we'd have to swallow to pull it off convincingly. Our most enduring country & western songs pay tribute to the good-hearted woman who lovingly welcomes her drunken, abusive man home each night after he's been whoopin' it up with the boys and dancing with loose women in honky-tonks.

While women were being taught to be submissive, men were receiving cultural messages instructing them to value their freedom above all else, and to beware of commitment, because it would inhibit that freedom. They also learned that a woman could become a castrating, nagging bitch if not properly subdued, and should that occur, the man would appear less manly to his peers. This of course, would be the worst of all catastrophes. And of course the ever-popular sexual double standard taught that men aren't naturally monogamous, so therefore cannot be expected to be faithful. Finally, since the beginning of human history, beating women (and even children) has not only been condoned, but *recommended*. Throw that all into the mix, and we have a very big problem on our hands.

Hopefully, few of us are still living in that world. For all of us, men and women, meeting, mating, and marrying is the most difficult of life's challenges. And once that part's handled, we still have to figure out how to get along after the dance of infatuation is over. The concept of balanced relationships between men and women, where the power is equally distributed, is brand new to human experience, which is why managing it is so hard. There are no precedents or traditions to rely on, and new rules are created daily.

By now, many of us have learned that if we don't deal fairly for ourselves we'll end up getting bulldozed into submission every time. Fortunately, society has changed a little, and women have been granted permission to act, more or less, as equals with men. The media tell us that we're now allowed to ask for dates, pay for dinner, initiate sex, and propose marriage. Yet when we come face-to-face with a new romance in real life, many of us still hesitate to seize power, fearing that it will make us look too aggressive. The idea of insisting on communication and commitment in a budding new relationship still sends intelligent women into a panic, fearing that they'll end up being seen as demanding, castrating, pushy shrews. We don't want to be seen as bitches and nags. At any cost.

Men are equally confused. They've heard rumors that women can now pay for dinner and initiate sex, but they're up against so many centuries of conditioning that it's hard—if not impossible—to change the patterns. On a radio talk show recently, I heard a discussion about an emerging new social trend. It appears that some man took some woman to dinner at an expensive restaurant for their first date. They decided that they weren't compatible, and agreed not to see each other again. He sent her a bill for half the cost of their dinner. It ended up in court.

The whole issue of equality is easy to deal with if you start with *communication*. This man and woman should have agreed in advance about who would pay for dinner. Communication is everything. There is no alternative. Here are some stories that illustrate how responsible communication can save us all a lot of time and heartache.

My friend Sue many years ago told me about her first encounter with her now husband, Jason. They had met in a bar, had some drinks, got along well, and when they said goodnight, he uttered those famous male words, *"I'll call you tomorrow."*

Sue, who'd recently graduated from a powerful self-improvement seminar, replied, "What time tomorrow?"

"In the morning," blinked an astonished Jason, putting on his jacket to leave.

"What time in the morning?" Sue negotiated. "I have a

busy day tomorrow, and I don't want to get hung up waiting to hear from you."

Uncomfortable but amused, Jason began to get the idea. "OK. How's nine o'clock?" he countered.

"Great," she said. "I'll talk to you then."

And at exactly 9:00 he called. The balance of power in their relationship was established.

When Sue told me this story back in 1981, I was stunned. "What a pushy woman!" I thought. "How could she pin him down like that when they didn't even have a relationship yet? How could she expect so much from him so early on?"

Expect so much? She was asking him only to respect her time by not making her wait for him, in much the same way he would respect the needs of his friends or business associates. But in my thinking, Sue might as well have been asking Jason to grab the moon out of the sky and gift-wrap it for her. My attitude said a lot about why I had so many unhappy relationships back then. And Sue's attitude says a lot about why she's been so successful in business as well as in her relationship with Jason.

In another, more typical scenario, the encounter would have gone down much differently. Sue could have accepted Jason's vague commitment to call her "tomorrow," and spent her day in deep anxiety, checking her answering machine obsessively or avoiding leaving her apartment altogether in case she'd miss his call. Women do this sort of thing. We learned it from our mothers, who learned it from *their* mothers. Boys and men were also taught a distinct set of rules, which were correlated to the women's rules. Do those of you (over 35) remember as teenagers your parents teaching you the rules of the game?

Little wonder the divorce rate skyrocketed in the 1970s, when the people who'd met and married under these rules finally began realizing they had no idea who they were, or whom they had married. Even though the guidelines of the 1950s seem archaic and quaint to us now, they are so deeply embedded into our social programming that they're hard to shake. In one way or another, many of us still operate according to these rules, or some variation of them.

I remember when Beth, an old roommate of mine, had just met her husband, Amos, in the early 1980s. They met on a Saturday, and he said he'd call her sometime during the week. By Thursday he hadn't called, and after waiting and wondering all week, Beth finally gave up and went to a rehearsal of the orchestra in which she played the flute. But before she left she asked me to baby-sit the phone for the evening (answering machines were uncommon back then), and instructed me to act surprised if he called, as if I'd never heard a word about him (I'd been hearing about nothing else all week). She begged me to "be cool."

He called. I acted cool. The game had begun. For the next several months of their courtship, he would always leave her with, "I'll call you." But he never said *when* he would call. Even though they spent most nights of the week together and neither was seeing anyone else, he never said, "I'll call you tomorrow" or "Let's have dinner at my place Wednesday." It was always "I'll call you." So Beth never made any other plans, because she never knew for sure if she'd be with him on any particular night. She had no life other than waiting around for Amos. And she suffered over this constantly.

These two examples from Sue and Beth illustrate opposite sides of the coin. Sue demanded a certain kind of treatment, and she got it. Beth was dating an immature, inconsiderate man (who she eventually married and later divorced), and made the mistake of not laying down the ground rules in the beginning. In their relationship, Beth never made demands on Amos for fear of losing him. So he never had a chance to learn about what she needed or wanted, and never saw her as someone who deserved to be treated with respect. He got the message that his behavior was acceptable, simply because she wouldn't tell him otherwise. She gave him permission to treat her badly.

Women are taught that men are delicate creatures. If we push them too hard, if we close the walls in around them, they'll run away and find someone else who will give them more "space." Men are taught that women are there to nurture and support them, like their mothers did (mom rarely asked for anything in return).

The sexual revolution had long-term positive effects, such as encouraging couples to separate rather than stay in stifling, loveless relationships, and freeing women to be sexual beings. But it was a painful transition. In my circle of friends (I was a tie-dyed, backpacked, communal-living hippie), it was considered unenlightened to admit to feeling jealousy. The politically correct behavior was to understand your lover's need to experience other people and give him or her the freedom to be or find him- or herself. Unfortunately, there was a double standard here: The women were doing most of the *understanding* and the men were doing most of the *experiencing*.

Once, back then, a girlfriend of mine caused shock waves through our crowd when she announced her engagement to a guy who had a reputation for being the most promiscuous and unattainable of all. We marveled at this feat, but she simply said, "I got a commitment because I insisted on it." We were flabbergasted. Here we were, afraid to ask our men for anything—to be faithful to us, to get a job, to take out the garbage—so afraid of being demanding and uptight like our mothers, that we ended up asking for, and getting, nothing at all.

It took a lot of years, a lot of boyfriends, and a lot of therapy before I learned how to get what I wanted—and deserved—in relationships. Eventually two miraculous things happened. The first was that I decided the pain of being alone was preferable to the pain of being with someone who broke my heart every other day. The second was the arrival of my now ex-husband, Jim—the perfect man at the time—into my life. *Without realizing it,* I automatically started playing by new rules from the moment we met (even though we're now divorced, we remain best of friends).

Jim and I met at a party, had a 15-minute conversation, exchanged phone numbers, and went our separate ways. I was intrigued by him and thought about him all night. The new rules went into effect the very next day, when I fearlessly called him at his office and said, more or less, this:

"I really enjoyed talking to you last night; it's rare to meet someone with a mind like yours, and I'd like to know you better. But I hate the games that go on between men and women. I hate the fact that I'm supposed to wait for you to call me, and that you may never call. I hate that routine, and I don't want to take that chance. So *I'm* calling *you* to see if you'd like to get together. Otherwise, the hell with it. I don't have time to play games."

His response (as he retold it to our friends many times over the years) was to wonder what he had done to make me so angry. He was completely caught off guard by my brutal honesty, because he was accustomed to doing it the old way. He'd been a classic ladies' man for the previous 20 years, guilty of every stereotypical male move in the book. He'd always chosen women who acted demure and submissive, which tilted the balance of power in his favor. My approach blew his whole game right out the window. Fortunately, he saw it as a challenge, and he accepted. Being thus challenged, butting heads with a woman who was a worthy opponent, was exactly what *at least part of him* had been looking for. Until then, he'd gotten bored with women who'd allowed themselves to be manipulated by him.

Dealing with people at that level of honesty requires taking enormous risks. But the goal is to make sure you come out of the encounter, the phone call, the date, or the affair with as little permanent scarring as possible. The risk is that you'll frighten the person away, and you'll find out he or she can't handle being as direct and clear about his or her intentions as you are. The alternative is to keep your real needs hidden, and to waste weeks, months, or a lifetime in a relationship that isn't based on truth. My marriage with Jim finally ended for the same reason it began. My independence and outspoken style, which had once been so appealing to him, after 8 years could no longer coexist with the part of him that still wanted someone demure and submissive.

In dating there are so many stages of judgment that we go through, and so much fear, that the pressure is almost unbearable. On the first date, we're afraid that we'll reveal too much about ourselves, and we'll be rejected. When we're that vulnerable, nothing hurts more that getting dumped because you didn't match someone's fantasy of the perfect partner. Later on, there's that first group outing or party where your new lover meets your friends for the first time. Will he or she pass the social test? Be too shy? Drink too much? Say something stupid? Belch loudly?

Then comes meeting the family. For some of us, the worst nightmares imaginable are conjured up here. We're afraid that when our lovers see us interacting with our parents, they'll see our worst demon—the powerless, beaten-down inner child who always seems to come out when we're with our families. It's a secret side of our personalities that we never want anyone to witness.

And then there's that point in a new relationship when one or both parties need to know where they stand in order to get on with their life. This is tough. I've seen people go crazy for months wondering when the right time was to ask these burning questions and make these presumptuous, terrifying statements:

> "I love you."
>
> "I want us to be monogamous."
>
> "Can we assume we'll be spending weekends together?"
>
> "Is there a future here?"
>
> "Here's some space in my closet to hang your clothes when you're here."

When it came to that point for Jim and me, when I desperately needed to determine whether or not we had an exclusive relationship, it happened in a very amusing way. We'd been together about 4 weeks, and during that time, he was still attempting to play a favorite game of his which we'd affectionately dubbed "holdout." Holdout meant he'd call me only every *other* day, and never make plans for the weekend until the last minute, though it was beginning to be understood that we always spent weekends together. I decided he'd been torturing me long enough, and it was time to put an end to it. I planned to talk to him about this on Friday night.

Several weeks earlier, *before we'd met,* I had planned an enormous party for the weekend after my scheduled show-down with Jim. The party had a theme and a name—the Human Swap Meet—and the idea was for everyone to bring a single, unattached friend of either sex for the purpose of introducing him or her around and doing some serious matchmaking. I had no way of knowing at the time that a few weeks later I'd have fallen in love with someone.

I had a real problem on my hands. Would I attend the party as an available female, or would Jim come with me, appearing in front of my friends as my new boyfriend, thereby letting everyone know that I was no longer available, and wiping out any opportunity I might have to meet someone else at the party? The only way to find out was to present my dilemma to him.

So there we were, in a restaurant, and I was very nervous because this was going to be one of those awful moments where I'd corner him into telling me the truth about his intentions. I was sweating bullets when I said, "I have to talk to you about something important."

"OK," he said casually.

I reached into my purse for the invitation to the Human Swap Meet, and presented it to him.

"Read this." An easy way out. The invitation would explain everything.

He read. Then he looked up at me with a sort of dumb-founded look on his face, and read some more. He was starting to look concerned.

"So, are you inviting me to this party?" he asked.

"Depends on you," I answered. I was *so* cool!

"And you want to know if I'm going to be there as your boyfriend, or if you'll be there as a participant in the swap meet?"

"That's right. If we're not, as they say, an item, then I'll be looking for someone else. If you go with me, then I won't be able to meet anyone at a party I planned for just that reason.

So it looks like we have to decide what we are. Before the end of the week."

"Hmmm," he said, slowly, torturing me again. "OK," he smiled. "Here's your answer. I'll be there, and I won't leave until you kick me out, which I hope will not happen in this lifetime."

Whammo! So *that* was his position. Exactly the answer I'd hoped for.

The point of all this is that *you have to ask.*

Variations on our conversation continued in many forms for several weeks, until we'd hammered out an agreement about what each of us wanted from the relationship. I told him "holdout" had to go, and he agreed to give it up. He told me I'd have to quit smoking, and I did. We agreed that spending every weekend together would be assumed. He gave me a key to his apartment, and said that I could use it anytime without having to worry about walking in on him with another woman. I told him I wouldn't wear high heels, which he loved, because they hurt my feet. He told me he would never cook a meal because that hurt *his* feet. We negotiated the terms of our relationship, the same way one might negotiate a business deal. It has to be done that way. And it can be renegotiated any time there's a need to reaffirm or change something.

When we're attracted to someone and we want him or her to love us, we want to give the impression that we're strong, that we're different from those who came before us, that we're totally self-sufficient and not the least bit dependent on another person to make us happy. We want to promise that we won't criticize our lovers or expect them to change for us. But those are impossible ideals to live up to. The more we try to convince our partners of how superhuman we are, the more they'll expect us to be superhuman.

We've all heard of (or been in) relationships where love blooms passionately for a short time (weeks, months), and then the lovers start to let their guards down. They start feeling more secure, so they begin to show who they really are, which looks different from what was originally presented. When we stop being on our best behavior and allow ourselves to drop the pretenses, things change. We stop dressing to please the other person (the fuzzy bunny slippers come out and the leather minidress disappears). We begin to talk more honestly about ourselves and our needs, and expect our partners to communicate the same way with us. That's what's supposed to happen in a real partnership.

Wouldn't it be easier if we simply started out that way in the beginning? If there were fewer pretenses to drop? Because if your dating life followed a few simple new rules—like *tell the truth, tell your whole story, take risks,* and *break rules*—your relationships would transform. You might wind up with fewer relationships, *but the ones you have will be the ones you want.* And this is true in every aspect of your life.

It's not an easy step to take. It takes intense psychological work to change the patterns that allow us to let someone lie to us repeatedly, break promises, and toy with our emotions. Sometimes it just takes getting hurt enough times until we simply refuse to take it anymore. So we need to change that list of old dating rules, one by one, so that they make sense for responsible, conscious women *and men* of today.

* * * * *

Girls' and Women's Dating Rules from the 1950s and 1960s

1. If you're interested in a boy, don't let him know. Wait for him to approach you. If he never does, movies and literature have taught us that it's noble and romantic to pine away for the unrequited love until we die.

2. Never, ever call a boy. Under any circumstances, *ever.*

3. On a date, never offer an opinion or suggest an activity. If he asks what you'd like to do, say, "Whatever you'd like to do." Men and boys need to know they're in control.

4. Don't go out with him on Saturday if he calls later than Wednesday (he'll think you're not popular if you're not booked weeks in advance). Tell him you're busy even if

it's a lie. It's better to spend Saturday night at home feeling miserable than to let a boy think you're too available.

5. Never go out on Saturday night with girlfriends, or everyone will know you couldn't get a date.

6. Never let him know that you're smarter than he is. Don't beat him at games.

7. If you show even the slightest interest in sex, he'll think you're cheap and he won't respect you. He'll use you for his disgusting animal needs, but he'll marry a *nice* girl. If you must allow petting, be sure he promises to marry you after graduation.

8. Don't talk about yourself or your problems.

9. Pretend to be interested in the things he likes, such as sports or cars, no matter how boring.

10. After you've been waiting all week for him to call, pretend to be out when he finally does, to show him how little you care.

*   *   *   *   *

*   *   *   *   *

Boys' and Men's Dating Rules from the 1950s and 1960s

1. Always pay for all dates (and don't complain about prices).

2. You are entitled to sex in return for an expensive date.

3. Never display weakness of any kind. Don't show your feelings if you're hurt or upset or even extremely happy. Be cool at all times.

4. Promise to call her, but don't call too soon or too often. It's best to keep her guessing.

5. Plan activities for the two of you in advance. Girls like being surprised, so it's good to be mysterious about what you're going to do. It makes you look strong and in control.

6. Never let your date catch you looking at other women.

7. Don't go out with fat, ugly, or unpopular women. Other men won't respect you.

8. Never date a woman smarter than you.

9. It is permissible to tell a girl you love her in order to score (in fact, tell her anything she wants to hear in order to score).

10. Never get serious with a girl who's too "easy."

*   *   *   *   *

*   *   *   *   *

Courtship Rules for Real People in the Real World

1. If you're interested in someone, let him or her know. Don't wait for your intended to read your mind and take a risk on approaching you. Take responsibility for what you feel, and communicate it as soon as you're sure. This avoids a lot of anguish, second-guessing, and wasted time.

2. Anybody can call anybody, anytime. If there's something you want to say, then call. You wouldn't hesitate to call a business associate or friend if you needed to talk. Why should it be more precarious with a lover or potential lover?

3. Participate fully in decision-making processes. There are two individuals at work here, each with something interesting and unique to offer, so let the ideas and suggestions flow freely. When two people agree on everything all the time it means that only one of them is doing the thinking.

4. Make up your own rules about planning and schedules. If you have a busy life, then you can't wait until Friday to make plans for Saturday. But if Friday rolls around and you still have no plans for the weekend, why not accept an invitation if it's something that appeals to you? The only rea-

son to decline should be because you're not interested, for whatever reason. Not because you're trying to save face.

5. Don't abandon your friends for your new love. Bring them together and spread love around!

6. Be proud of your intelligence, experience, and wisdom. It's what makes you fascinating and desirable to other people. If the person you're dating is threatened by that, then find someone new who will love you for it.

7. The old rules about sex are behind us, but there are new rules now, and they're important. Sex is for increasing communication, not for manipulation or power games. Be honest about when and how you want to do it. And *both of you* are equally responsible for birth control and disease prevention.

8. Talk about everything. Reveal yourself completely. The goal is for you to get to know each other. There's no time for guessing games.

9. Be open to the other person's interests, but don't deny your own. If he's into deep-sea fishing and you're into opera, think of how much fun it could be to introduce each other to these strange new worlds. But set limits. Don't go fishing with him if you're going to hate every minute of it. Instead, spend the afternoon doing something you like while he's out at sea. *It's OK to have two lives.*

10. Always take phone calls, even if it's just to say, "I'm not interested in going out with you." It's just plain rude to ignore someone who's sincerely trying to communicate.

*　　*　　*　　*　　*

About Workplace Romances

I'm a big believer in acknowledging *mutual* love wherever you find it. There are no taboos between consenting adults. Many of us are so obsessed with our careers, so brainwashed about loyalty to our jobs, so addicted to the money or the approval of our superiors, that we forget to live our own lives. Love is the most important thing there is. Your job pales in comparison.

These days, the workplace is one of the best spots for single people to meet one another. It's not like it was in the old days when women stayed home doing needlepoint while men went out into the world. If I was single, I'd want to spend my days in the middle of the largest corporate office tower on earth surrounded by as many eligible *and employed* men as possible. Or the largest construction site. Or a large hospital full of rich doctors. Or on the road with a rock band. No matter what kind of workplace it is, it's a safe and legitimate hunting ground.

If you find love on the job, then jump right in. But like all other things in your life, remember to be honest. You can hide it for a while, until you know if it's serious. But then you have to bring it out of the closet. The odds are that your boss and your coworkers will be happy for you, but if they're not, then you have to decide if the relationship is more important than the job. If you both see a future, then it's worth changing jobs for. After all, a relationship is supposed to change your life. Love is supposed to move you forward and wake you up. Not keep you asleep.

Sex and the Image You Project

I'm often asked for advice on how to get past the sex barrier in social situations. Businesswomen with only business on their minds complain of being constantly hit on by lusty gentlemen at business functions. Men with only the most honorable of intentions feel they're not taken seriously when initiating conversations with females, because the women are on guard against lusty gentlemen. How do you know whom to trust? How do you know who's being real?

The answer lies in the question, Are *you* being real?

Before you begin a program of aggressive socializing, you should be very clear and very honest with yourself about your goals. Subconscious messages come through loud and clear sometimes, no matter how well we think we're hiding them. You might be attending a business conference to advance your career, but if in your heart you're hoping for a romantic fling, you can't hold it against someone who picks up on your subconscious message and responds accordingly. We humans are more psychic than we give ourselves credit for. Look carefully at the messages you may be sending.

Ladies, if you don't want to be seen as a sex object at the annual meeting of the American Association of Hospital Administrators, then leave the miniskirt and 4-inch heels at home. On the other hand, it's perfectly all right to go to the meeting with mating on your mind, as long as you're honest with yourself and others about why you're there. It isn't fair to wonder why men are coming on to you when you claim you're only there for business but you're dressed for seduction.

Men, if your conversation with that attractive female sales rep is really about ordering 100 cases of paper for your copy machine, then there's no reason the conversation shouldn't go smoothly. But if you're fantasizing about having sex with her, making sexual innuendoes or looking at her chest rather than her eyes, then can you really blame her for treating you with disdain? What if it's the other way around, and *she's* coming on to *you*? Are the rules different when a man is the target of an unwanted sexual advance by a woman? No. The rules are for same for both sides, and, as always, it's based on truthful communication.

Reasonably intelligent and conscious people *can read each other's minds*. You're completely responsible for what you bring into a room, and for what you project onto other people. So if it's a business function, *and you're there strictly for business,* then act appropriately. Believe in yourself as a businessperson, and other people will believe you too. If they aren't buying it, then take a look at yourself to find out why.

Flirting can be harmless and delightful and can always be used to your advantage, whether for social or business purposes, if it's done within reason. But it can also be used for the wrong reasons—to wield power, to hurt someone, or to seek approval. If there's a part of you that wants to flirt brazenly, then let that part come forth freely and without denial. Just be aware that there may be consequences. You're responsible for the messages you send, and you can't complain if others pick up on your cues. On the other hand, if you're serious about wanting to be left alone and are still attracting suitors, one good defensive move is to buy an imitation wedding band and wear it to the functions in which you're all business.

If you're socializing with your spouse or intimate partner, there are some boundaries to consider. In a committed relationship where sexual exclusivity has been agreed upon, it's rude and downright cruel to flirt overtly with someone else, to make sexual innuendoes, or to act in a sexual way toward another person. If you're sending sexual messages out to others in a way that makes your partner uncomfortable, even if you have no wish for a sexual encounter, then you need to examine your own personal truth. Are you unhappy with your relationship? Are there issues, sexual or otherwise, that need to be addressed between you and your partner? Many times we act seductive out of insecurity and a need for reassurance. But it can cause a lot of pain and conflict for the ones we love. It's a matter of etiquette, and a matter of honoring your relationship. But most of all, it's about your emotional needs and finding healthy ways to meet them.

If you *are* out to attract lovers, then go all the way with it. Be the sexiest, warmest, funniest, most attractive person in the room. No matter what it is you're looking for, if truth is the foundation of your communication, then you're going to find it.

Body Language

In 1970, Julius Fast published a book called *Body Language* in which people learned to read one another's subconscious messages by observing the way they positioned their bodies and body parts. Looking back at this book, it's quaint that the author referred to women as "girls" and described body language using mostly scenarios in which men were trying to seduce them.

Now that women have been liberated (somewhat) from this kind of thinking, the information is even more useful than it was back then. Both women and men need to understand body language so that they can radiate clear messages to one another, whether for business or for pleasure. The whole idea of body language can be summed up neatly by remembering one basic rule: *Sexual body language excludes others in the room, while nonsexual body language does not.* Sexual body language closes your conversation off so that it includes only the two of you. Nonsexual body language keeps your circle of conversation open, and positions you as part of the group, rather than in a private huddle.

Many of us are familiar with Fast's concepts, but here's a rundown in case you've forgotten:

Sexual Body Language

- Leaning in closely to the person you're speaking with, which creates a closed circle.

- Speaking in quiet, intimate tones which discourage others from joining your conversation.

- Touching the other person or touching your own body, including clothes, hair, or jewelry.

- Eliminating references to other people or the outside world from the conversation.

- Facing the other person and looking directly into his or her eyes.

Nonsexual Body Language

- Sitting up straight instead of leaning forward.

- Facing your body toward the room rather than directly toward the other person.

- Speaking loudly enough so that others can hear you and join the conversation if they wish.

- In the context of your conversation, referring to other people in the room, or referring to people who are in a position of authority. ("Your wife is traveling in Greece this week? How interesting! My boss, Mr. Dithers, went to Greece last year.")

- Respecting physical boundaries by not touching the other person and leaving sufficient space between you.

You are free to choose behaviors from either side of the spectrum, depending on the response you want to get. Once you realize that you have a choice about what to express, you can abandon many of the old rules of polite behavior and replace them with new ones. Good little boys and girls may not get in trouble very often, but they don't have much fun either.

Job Hunting and
the Workplace

Until now, you've been reading about how independent entrepreneurial types prospect for new business contacts. But what about those of us who are employed by others, who work nine to five and can't schmooze on company time or print our newsletters on the office computer? When the time comes to look for greener employment pastures, the majority of us are limited during business hours because our time is controlled by somebody else.

Schmoozing for Jobs

If you're a full-time employee of a company, there are still ways that you can network as much as someone who is self-employed. In fact, there may be hidden benefits, not the least of which is that your employer may pick up the tab for the events you attend as a representative of your company. While it may not be the epitome of loyalty to network on your own behalf at these events, it is most certainly acceptable if you do it with a little tact and diplomacy. If you're a sales rep for a wallpaper company, and you go to the annual convention of the Western Wallpaper Association at your company's expense, you're in prime territory to scout around for a better job. You can do it with dignity—and without embarrassing or angering the company you work for—by using the same techniques for starting conversations and handing out business cards that we've talked about so far. But be aware that there are two very different groups you'll be dealing with.

1. Your Peers

Peers are the people who have jobs similar to yours and who can provide an excellent network for you. Tell every one of them that you're looking for a new job and ask them to keep an ear to the ground for you. Hand out cards and résumés, and follow up on all leads and suggestions offered. You can be honest about your intentions with the people in this group.

But stay away from those who might be in direct competition with you *for your current job*. Don't give them the ammunition to undermine or blackmail you because they know you're considering leaving the company.

2. Your Employer's Peers

Your employer's peers have the power to hire you, but they require a much more subtle approach. Remember that you want to impress them with your commitment to your work, your loyalty, and your competence, so you'll have to follow a few rules.

The most important thing to remember about talking to your boss's peers at social events is that you should not pitch them directly for a job. Instead, simply make contacts that you can use later on when you're ready to aggressively start your job-seeking campaign. Make friends with them. Sit next to them at dinner and have a conversation about sports, politics, or anything else they appear to be enthusiastic about. Find or create common ground by acting like an equal. Get their business cards. At the end of the evening, you'll have an ally, a new friend, and a good contact. You can hit them up for a job later.

Never say anything bad about the company or the person you currently work for. Instead, try to get your prospect to reveal *her* impressions of your company. If this creates an opportunity to indicate that you'll soon be available, then by all means, let it be known. If not, then stay in the conversation and impress your prospect with your knowledge of the business and your ability to do your job. And above all, relate to her as an equal—two real human beings having a conversation. She'll become a valuable contact for the future.

You can network for a job anywhere, any time. It's perfectly acceptable to tell new people that you meet that you're currently "between jobs," or "considering new options." For some of us, it may be embarrassing to reveal something as personal as the fact that we're unemployed, because we think that it somehow puts our status at risk. But remember all the rules we've been talking about—how telling the truth and telling your whole story actually puts you at an advantage—and accept the possibility that each time you're too embarrassed to tell someone you're job hunting, you've missed an opportunity for a new lead or some useful information that can benefit your search. At the risk of having someone decide you're not worth talking to because you're unemployed (not terribly likely), try speaking up. If you do, doors will open that otherwise would have remained closed.

Job Interviews

I once participated in a panel presentation for a group called Los Angeles Advertising Women. The topic was "How to Get Ahead in the Job Market," and the audience was comprised of account executives, production people, and media buyers (these titles in the advertising world are the equivalent of middle management in the general business world). Almost all those in the audience were either unemployed or dissatisfied with their current positions, and they were hungry for information on how to make their next moves.

The panel featured recruitment specialists, personnel people, and me, an expert on networking. As the evening progressed and the panelists answered questions from the audience about résumés and interviewing techniques, it became pretty clear that my perspective was different from everyone else's. For example, a recruitment person said that one way to make a good impression during an interview is to research the company, its activities, and its management style, and convince the interviewer not only that you know a lot about the firm but that you can fit neatly into its corporate culture. When the same question was directed to me, my answer took a lot of people by surprise.

"Be yourself. Tell the truth about who you are. Let your personality and energy come forth, and let your ability to clone yourself into a worker drone be secondary."

"Gasp!" went the room.

I continued by saying things like, "If you're not hired for who are, you won't be respected for who you are when you're working there, and you won't be happy in the job. If you like to wear cowboy boots, don't interview for a job that makes formal business attire absolutely mandatory. If your politics are passionately liberal, don't expect to be happy in a conservative company that makes large donations to the Republican Party. It won't work. In job interviews, it's vitally important to tell the truth about who you are."

The panel presentation continued along those lines, and when it was over, I was surrounded by animated job seekers thanking me for my unconventional wisdom. Almost all of them told me that my off-center philosophy echoed their own, but they were afraid to really act on such ideas.

Breaking traditional rules is something that works in job hunting as well as in socializing. And it's something that must be done if you're going to stand up and be noticed.

Don't be a résumé. Be a person. With a personality. Don't be afraid to reveal a little more about yourself. In the 1990s, corporate conformity and formality are on the wane. A recent study showed that companies which gave their employees "casual days" (1 day per week where they could come to work in jeans) found that employee productivity was better on those days. Some companies took the experiment a bit further and abolished dress codes altogether, trusting that employees would be smart enough to dress with taste. They found that employee morale and productivity soared when people were allowed to express their individuality.

Those who are willing to take risks by following their hearts and their instincts usually find a far more rewarding experience in the workplace than those who worry about second-guessing the boss every day. Telling the truth to yourself, and *living it,* makes for a much more interesting life. And taking responsibility for the decision to be that way will ultimately position you within a group of friends, coworkers, or extended family who will accept and respect you for the stand you've taken.

There's only one rule in life that really works all the time, and it's the one about being true to thine own self.

* * * * *

How to Make Better Contacts (and Better Impressions) When Job Hunting

1. Have your local computer service bureau remodel and print your résumé so that it looks clean and professional, but also creative enough to stand out from the crowd. Then attach a warm, naturally worded, typed cover letter—not a stiff, formal letter that lacks personality.

2. When you've chosen a company you like, find out what social events it hosts and get yourself invited. Find out what sports or charities the company bigwigs participate in, and get involved in them. If the executives are there, other smart employees will be too, and you may be able to make contact with them. Make friends first; probe for openings later.

3. Attend events listed in the local calendar of your newspaper or industry trade magazine that relate to your chosen company's interests—especially daytime luncheons—and aggressively work the room before and after the program.

4. If you interview with a company and fall in love with it, let people know. Not by pleading for a job, but by following up with calls, letters, and stand-out actions, like sending an invitation to a party or event *you're* hosting. There's a fine line between effective follow-up and *pestering,* a line that may take some experimentation. But unless you're sure you've aced the interview, there's great wisdom in the saying, "Act like a winner and you'll be treated like one."

5. Be an original! These days, as opposed to the 1950s, when a prospective employee's ability to conform was his most prized asset, employers are looking for people who show a spark of life, a personality, a direction. Men, why not show your personality by wearing an artistic tie? Women, wear a bright tropical print or rare antique blouse under your conservative black suit. Don't be so polite that you come across as dull.

6. Use normal language on your résumé. Avoid this kind of résumé-speak:

"In this entry-level position, my duties included supervision of administrative staff, correspondence, and interfacing with upper management."

Yuck! Try saying that out loud to yourself in the mirror. It's pretty silly isn't it? It's not the way people really talk. It's stiff, awkward, boring, and unoriginal. And it doesn't give much information about what you did at that job. Does anybody really ever say the word "interfacing"? Next time, try writing it as if it were something you'd say in everyday conversation. Like this:

"In this position, I supervised a staff of six who handled basic clerical tasks. I was in touch with our clients and suppliers daily about customer service and purchasing questions, and worked with them to develop consumer promotions for our products. I also consulted with upper management on new marketing strategies and other business development activities."

*   *   *   *   *

The Art of Follow-Up: Getting Through the Blackout Periods

So now you can work a room with confidence and ease. You've been practicing the everyday dress rehearsals; and you've begun to actually enjoy talking to people in elevators and in line at the grocery store. You've even become adept at introducing yourself to strangers, making interesting conversation, telling your whole story, and getting others to tell theirs. You've made a commitment to becoming an effective, aggressive schmoozer, and you work hard at it by going to parties, meetings, conventions, and lectures, and talking to everyone about everything. You've given out your printed propaganda—brochures, flyers, business cards—and you've collected the same from the people you've met. Good work! You've just mastered 50 percent of the job.

Every day we meet new people who interest us, though we may not be sure why, or what the potential is. We just know that we want to keep them around, so we exchange phone numbers or business cards as a way of saying, "I find you interesting enough to let you know how to reach me should you decide you'd like to in the future." The key word here is *future,* and the secret to building these new people into your life over the long-term is *follow up*.

There are two things you can do with all the business cards and phone numbers you collect from the people you meet:

1. Hope that all the people you handed your card to will call *you*.
2. Map out a specific, long-term strategy for keeping in touch with them.

The second approach is a lot of work, which is why most people don't choose it. Those who do, succeed. The rest sit around and wonder why their lives haven't happened yet.

The best follow-up occurs over a long period of time without expectation of immediate results. Not everyone you meet will like you, need your services, or have a reason to pursue a relationship with you on the spot. But if there was a spark there, some strong interest or attraction, a common purpose or potential for something in the future, you're going to want to hold on to these people.

Let's say you've just met a hot prospect, someone who's about to begin a project in which there could be opportunities for you. Perhaps he's opening a new division of his company in your part of town and may have a job for you. Or maybe it's someone who's starting a new business and will need you, a computer consultant, to set up a network for her staff. Maybe it's a potential mate who's in the process of trying to gracefully exit another relationship. The possibilities are limitless. But in these situations, the prospect isn't ready to make a commitment yet, and may not be for several months, or even years. Maybe his new division won't be hiring until the spring, or her new business won't have the budget for a computer system until the end of the year.

Although there's no immediate gratification on the horizon for you here, these people are *keepers*. Keepers are the people you want to stay close to for any number of reasons. Perhaps they're incredibly interesting, and you had such a good rapport with them when you first met that you'd like to permanently build them into your social life. Or perhaps you want them to consider you when they're ready to make a decision that might include you, but there's no immediate action you can take. How do you keep connected?

If you wait 6 months and then call out of the blue hoping

you'll be remembered, both of you run the risk of being greatly embarrassed by fuzzy-memory syndrome. Instead, you need to develop a long-term follow-up plan that includes ongoing contact through letters, newsletters, greeting cards, invitations, phone calls, or other communications. You not only will remain visible, but will slowly cultivate this person into a friend or business associate.

I recently met a woman who told me a remarkable story about a situation in which long-term follow-up paid off. She was president of a small company that supplied and serviced sophisticated megacomputers for large organizations like universities, hospitals, utility companies, and the military. She'd been going after a specific government account for a long time—7 years to be exact. Over and over again, she'd watch her competitors get the contracts that she had bid at a lower price, while her communications and presentations would be systematically ignored. Out of sheer tenacity, year after year, she refused to give up. And then one day, she'd had enough.

She sat down and wrote what she described to me as a final "surrender letter," not to the man in charge of computer purchasing, who'd been rejecting her for so long, but to his boss. The letter basically said, "I give up. I've been pursuing your company for 7 years. I've underbid my competitors with packages containing far more quality and better service, to no avail. It's become clear to me that your director of computer purchasing is unwilling to deal with a minority-owned business, so I hereby throw in the towel, and will not be calling on you anymore."

Amazingly, that letter blew the doors of the company wide open. Within a week, the head honcho himself called her and informed her that the purchasing director she'd been dealing with for the last 7 years had just been fired, and that he would be most interested in her making a presentation to the new director. She did, and won the account that afternoon.

Most people wouldn't spend 7 years pursuing a particular lead. Many people don't even stay in business that long. Granted, this is an extreme example, but it illustrates how important certain uncontrollable factors can be, like timing.

There's only one way to guarantee that you'll stay in the running through innumerable sets of ever-changing circumstances, and that's to *stick with it*.

At any moment, a company can make a sudden change in personnel, budgets, marketing strategies, location, product line, or management style. If one of these changes happens to occur on the day that your letter or sales package arrives, you've got a fresh start. Here are examples of follow-up methods that can be used in a variety of situations.

The Business Follow-Up Letter

Consider sending a short letter to someone with whom you had a business-related conversation—for example, the woman who needed help with her new computer network. You can remind her that you were interested in the project that was discussed, and use it as an opportunity to present additional information about yourself, such as a brochure or client list. Here's a follow-up letter to the successful, hard-to-reach real estate developer I met for a moment at a recent trade show:

Mr. Jay Goldblum
Big Real Estate Honcho
Beverly Hills, CA 90210

Dear Jay:

As promised when we met at the Home Restoration Show, I've enclosed some information on my firm and on some of the real estate clients we've served. I've also included examples of the kinds of articles and other press coverage that we can generate with an ongoing PR program.

1. A *Los Angeles Times* article about my client Otis Elmont predicting the arrival of the push-button home.

2. *Entrepreneur Magazine* "corporate profiles" on two of my clients, Edmond Davis and Marianne Levine of ADR Financing. Positioning company principals as experts in their fields is an important part of developing a high profile for the company.

3. A *Los Angeles Business Journal* article, written by my
   client Chris Hill of Hill, Brown & Stoumen Architects,
   based on a position paper issued by his firm. The article
   was published in nine consumer and trade publications,
   and has brought the firm inquiries from as far away as
   South America and Italy.

There are, of course, a variety of other PR activities that can
be developed to increase public awareness for your company.
Special events, press conferences, and promotional tie-ins
with related products are just a few, which, when supported
by continued distribution of news releases, provide a steady
stream of information to the press about your company's
activities.

I'll call you later in the week to see if you'd like to schedule
a meeting to view a portfolio of our work. I look forward to
speaking with you then.

Best regards,

The Personal Follow-Up Letter

Use a personal follow-up letter to acknowledge the fact that
someone made a memorable impression on you, and that you
wish to stay in touch. It's not a sales pitch, but a friendly show
of support. These letters can be to an author you met whose
work you admire, a colleague in your business, or an interesting person of any kind whom you wish to keep as an acquaintance or friend:

Oscar Janiger
The Albert Hoffman Foundation
Dear Oscar:

I very much enjoyed our conversation at the Bentleys'
Christmas party last week. Your work with LSD therapy is
fascinating, and a subject I've followed closely for many
years. It's a project that's been a long time coming, and I'm
delighted that someone with your knowledge and vision has
taken it on. If there's any way in which I can support your

efforts, please call and let me know. My home number is 555-1968.

Meanwhile, I've added your name to my mailing list, and will keep you informed of any interesting news and information on the subject that comes my way.

I'd also like to invite you to the annual New Year's Day brunch that I host each year. An invitation is enclosed. You'll find quite a collection of interesting people there.

I hope to see you then!

This last letter is filled with important information. I called it a personal letter, but it can also double as a business letter, only with a slightly warmer touch. Take note of the elements it contains.

The opening sentence reminds him of where we met and the fact that we had a conversation about a particular subject. I restate my interest in the subject, and then offer my support in an open-ended way, which can mean either doing business with him or pursuing a social relationship. I tell him that I've added his name to my mailing list, letting him know that I plan to stay in touch. Giving him my personal home number indicates special attention. I then back that up with an invitation to a party, creating an opportunity for us to meet again, or for me to expect a return invitation of some kind from him in the future.

While personal and business follow-up letters can certainly be effective, they can't do all the work on their own. Don't give up if your first follow-up letter doesn't draw a response. It may take several attempts over a period of weeks or months to get someone's attention.

A client of mine who had limited funds scraped together enough money to print a beautiful brochure that she sent to 700 prospects with a short cover letter introducing the service she was offering. Two weeks after she mailed the brochures, she made follow-up calls to about 100 of the people on her list. Of those, 4 indicated some interest and asked her to call them again at a later date to set up a meeting.

But she was not happy about the results. She came to my

office upset, demanding to know why her brochures hadn't been effective enough. I explained to her (as I had 20 times before) that the way to get a response to any kind of marketing communication is to create multiple impressions. The prospects need to be exposed to the information several times before they really pay attention to it. That's why in advertising it usually makes more sense to buy four small ads running once per month in a magazine than one large ad which would appear only one time. I told her that the hard part of her solicitation was only just beginning, and that 4 interested prospects out of 100 was actually an excellent response for her first time out. Now, she needed to pursue those 4 people vigorously with calls and other mailed materials.

Of course you can't send the same letter time after time, so the trick is to come up with variations. One such variation is a newsletter.

Newsletters

Newsletters are the most effective way I know of to stay in touch with people in the outer circle of your friends, acquaintances, and associates. Keeping the inner circle intact is easy—these are the people you talk to daily, weekly, or even monthly. But what about the people around the edges? The ones you don't know very well (yet), or the ones you speak to only once per year? If you don't keep these contacts warm, they'll disappear.

My husband, Michael, after a 20-year career as an entertainment industry photographer, took a 2-year leave in 1993. During this time, he lost touch with a lot of his friends and clients, and when he was ready to resurface, he had to round them all up again. He did this by sending a newsletter which he called *Michael's Missive*, an informal two-page, newspaper-style letter which he sent to about 200 contacts. Two days after it was mailed, the phone started to ring with social invitations, job offers, and old friendships ready to be rekindled.

Another amazing newsletter story comes from my life with my former husband, Jim. For years we sent a newsletter to our friends and business associates. When we decided to adopt a baby in 1990, we put an item in the newsletter saying that we were looking for a child to adopt, and if anyone had any leads, to please let us know. We immediately got a call from a friend who knew a couple with a pregnant 24-year-old daughter who was looking for a home for her baby. That's how we found our son, Danny.

There's a funny follow-up to this story. Several years after that, when Jim and I separated, we sent out the "final" edition of our newsletter, announcing our pending divorce, and telling our friends that things were civil between us and that they didn't have to take sides. One of the recipients of this newsletter was a photographer I'd worked with in the past, a man named Michael Jacobs. When he got the newsletter, he called me to say hello and to talk about his own recent divorce. Soon after that we got together, and he's now the love of my life and my new husband. He's also a big believer in newsletters.

A newsletter can be anything from a one-page typed personal letter (the kind that many families send to friends and relatives at Christmas) to a four-color, 16-page glossy magazine. The family-style letter is fine for families, but in the business world newsletters serve as a marketing tool, so they should look and act more sophisticated and polished. The contents should include news about you, your business, and some of your personal activities. The newsletter can be as formal or casual as you like, depending on your personal style, the nature of your business, and the attitudes of the people who'll be receiving it.

Some newsletters are written in an informal, humorous style, targeted to a wide audience that includes both business associates and personal friends. Others are strictly business, written and designed in a more conservative fashion. While the style of your newsletter depends completely on who you are and the image you want to convey to your readers, there are some rules that apply across the board, and should be followed no matter what kind of newsletter you produce:

1. It should be very well written. If you aren't a writer, don't attempt to write your own newsletter (unless it's family-style). If your letter is going to business contacts and prospects, by all means hire a professional writer!

2. It should be well designed, in an easy-to-read format with typefaces that encourage comprehension. Use headlines, titles, subheadings, bullet points, and other elements to break up paragraphs of text. Graphics or photos are a plus. These details are best left to professional designers, so again, if you're not experienced at it, hire a copywriter *and* a designer.

3. The content should not be overly personal, overly detailed, or dull. Know your market. Give them information they'll respond to. For business, use news about your latest projects or sales figures, company events (awards, promotions, picnics), news about staff members (births, weddings), or trends in your industry. For letters that include both business and personal readers, you can write about the house you just bought, the charity you're volunteering for, or new films, products, or local restaurants you recommend.

My own personal newsletter is called *The Mandell Schmoozeletter*. It's a simple, inexpensive, easy-to-produce letter that combines personal and business news in a fun, upbeat writing style. My business in Los Angeles is a very informal one; we wear jeans and T-shirts to the office. My clients also tend to be casual types, so in my newsletter I can get away with being informal and personal in the content of its stories. It's written in the third person ("Michael and Terri Buy Land in Arizona") and designed in a newspaper-style layout, with bold headlines, and lines dividing each article. The articles cover both business and personal news from my life, and might include a story about my son's recent birthday and an article about the publication of this book.

Most newsletters are not as lighthearted as mine, but because the *Schmoozeletter* goes to a range of people with whom I have either very close relationships (family and friends) or informal business relationships (certain clients), I can get away with using a loose, conversational style.

At the other end of the spectrum, a newsletter published by a bank or an ad agency would have a very different style. It would be filled with photos of people in business attire giving presentations or talking at a conference table. It would be written in more formal language, and focus on industry trends, marketing techniques, and other information designed to pull in clients.

You wouldn't necessarily send this type of newsletter to friends and family, though you certainly could if you wanted to keep them informed about what's going on in your business. Its primary use is as a marketing tool, distributed to past *and* present clients, potential clients, and anyone else to whom you'd like to promote your business.

All these examples are very different from one another, and there is a world of possibilities in between. The beauty of having a newsletter is that it can do double-duty schmoozing. It not only can be used as a mailed follow-up piece after you've met someone new, but also can be carried with you to be handed out to people as an adjunct to your business card. Many people carry their newsletters with them wherever they go, so that they'll have something memorable to leave with any prospects they happen to meet.

Other Ways to Communicate

Business or personal follow-up letters and newsletters can cover a lot of ground. But don't necessarily expect a response from them. Remember that follow-up is a long-term process, so after you've sent your first letter, wait a month and then send something else. Keep your eyes open for interesting news articles or events related to your prospect's interests. If you happen to know, for example, that your prospect is a collector of African art, become aware of news and events related to that subject. Look in the Sunday calendar section of your daily newspaper for upcoming performances, exhibits, and shows. If you hear about an exciting new travel program that offers affordable trips to East Africa, make a note of it. Then send a very short cover letter (with a copy of the article or item) saying, "I thought you might be interested in seeing this. Hope all is going well for you."

Throughout the year, you can send all kinds of little tidbits, like your newsletter, an announcement of your new address, a birth announcement for your new baby, your brochure, a holiday greeting card, and of course invitations to parties and events. After your prospects have heard from you two or three times in this way, they'll know who you are. That's when you can call them on the phone to ask how the project is going and set up a meeting for your presentation or interview.

Assuming your messages have been sincere and professional, you should find a warm welcome waiting on the other end of the line for you. Because you have done no less than *reveal* yourself to someone new, who will most likely respect and admire your efforts, not to mention be flattered by them. But keep in mind that not everyone on your list is going to be a Power Schmoozer like you, and despite your best efforts, there will be times when you'll be ignored. Some people are just plain bad at communicating, and though they may appreciate your interest, they may never respond, simply because it's not their style, or their choice, to reach out and connect with people. Whatever you do, *don't take it personally,* and if you're inclined to continue your pursuit, by all means, go ahead. It's entirely possible that it will pay off eventually.

Keeping Track of Everything and Everyone

Before you can begin an effective follow-up program, you need a system for keeping track of everybody—ideally, a computer with a database program that manages mailing lists. If you don't have a computer, you can do it by hand—the old-fashioned way in a rolodex or card file—simply by keeping track of names, addresses, and information about the people you meet. Any way you do it, be sure to keep it current. Whenever you meet someone of interest, get his or her business card or address, and add it to the list.

My personal mailing list began in 1987 when I was putting together the guest list for my wedding. After the wedding, I realized I had the names and addresses of all my friends in my database, so I kept adding to it. It now contains about 500 names, including all my friends, family, clients, and miscellaneous people of interest that I collect as I go about my life. I have another mailing list as well, which contains the names and addresses of everyone who has ever attended my Power Schmoozing seminar. I stay in touch with them by keeping them informed of special projects, lectures, presentations, and events in which I'm involved. (If you'd like to be on this list, fill out the form at the back of this book and send it to me at the address given.)

Once you have a mailing list and a follow-up system, you'll wonder how you ever survived without it. With practice, it becomes easy to maintain. Some of the people on my lists I've only met once and may never see again, but they still get my newsletter every time I send it out. Some live in another state or another country, but that's OK, because I might visit that state or country someday. Some are old boyfriends, former teachers, the parents of the kids at my son's school, neighbors, clients, my accountant, and my dentist. I keep in touch with them all. And most of them seem to enjoy hearing from me.

Common Problems and What to Do About Them

Everybody has his or her own way of avoiding confrontation with personal demons. If your demons include the fear of changing your life, you've probably used every imaginable excuse a thousand times. But that's just what they are—excuses—and justifiable as they may seem, underneath each one is a fear. Changing them is just a matter of establishing new priorities. But don't worry if it seems impossible to change them immediately. You don't have to. As you change your priorities about what's important to you, such as making Power Schmoozing an important activity in your life, the obstacles will start to fall away on their own. Because no matter how you acquired your personal obstacles, you have the power to make them go away.

Problems Getting Motivated

For every reason you can come up with to avoid going out there and making contact, there is an equally valid solution. Here are some of the most overused, Oscar-winning excuses known to humankind for preventing your own networking success.

"I Can't Afford to Go to These Events"

You're right. Many of the best events can be a real hardship on your wallet. But there are ways to get around that.

1. Set up a networking fund—anywhere from $20 to $50 per month, or more if you can afford it. Make it a little reward for yourself in honor of something special you've done that month. Each month, you'll be able to attend a luncheon meeting of a professional organization, a charity fundraiser, charity events, or a special community event.

2. Offer to provide some kind of service to the organizations hosting the events that interest you, in exchange for the price of admittance. Or become a regular volunteer for your favorite organizations that host parties, receptions, meetings, and other events.

3. Check event listings and local community calendars for free or very low-cost events.

4. Ask your employer to allow you to attend business events as a representative of the company, at the company's expense. Once you get there, you can schmooze on behalf of the company, and on your own behalf as well.

"I Hate Going Places Alone"

Me too. Until I get there and start meeting interesting new people. Here's how to get past this one:

1. If you can't bear the idea of a solo outing, bring your cousin, your mother, your secretary, a coworker, a neighbor, or your kids (but call first to make sure it's OK to bring them).

2. Practice getting over your fear of going places alone by going somewhere with a friend, and then separating once you arrive. You'll get used to the reality of being there alone, but you'll know that your friend is nearby if you need her. Or go alone, but plan to have your friend meet you there later. Or just take a risk and fly solo. Going places alone is important, because in many situations, you'll do much better having the freedom to move around without having to "take care of" somebody else. It also makes you a more approachable target for other schmoozers.

"It's Not Safe in That Part of Town at Night"

It's appalling that women can't travel freely through our cities without being attacked. So while you're volunteering to help fight crime in your neighborhood (start a neighborhood watch group for added networking potential), try some of these solutions to make going out alone less of a risk:

1. Ask the organizers of the event if parking is close by. If not, ask if there are security personnel available to escort women from the parking lot to the venue.
2. Take a large male friend with you, or go in a group. Or take a self-defense course, or carry a stun gun (check local ordinances).
3. Call the organizers and ask them to consider having their next meeting at a better location. In fact, try giving them some ideas for better locations. You might even be able to get involved with the group by volunteering to help solve this problem.

"I Hate All the People in the (_____) Business— They Drink Too Much and They Smell Bad"

Well then, maybe it's time to find a new career! If you really dislike the people in your industry, then find a career with people you *do* like. (If this sounds a little oversimplistic, it's because most good solutions are.) Do you have a dream, an idea, a hobby, or career that you'd like to pursue but you don't know where to start? Start from scratch! Go to an event that has nothing at all to do with your current business and see what happens.

Are you a shoe salesman who's always wanted to be a writer? Contact the Publishers' Marketing Association or the Society of Authors and Journalists and go to one of their dinner meetings. (You can find these groups in the *Encyclopedia of Associations* at your local library.) Start getting to know their world, and meet the people who are active in it. Ask questions. Tell them about yourself and your goals. Once you take those first baby steps, everything else will start gathering its own momentum.

"I Never Know What to Talk to People About"

Arrive prepared. Read up on the organization and its activities. Get familiar with the speaker and the work he or she is doing. Arm yourself with information on current cultural or political events that might be of interest to the people in the room. Learn something about the location of the event, such as the history of the building, the new parking lot proposed for the site across the street, or the famous chef in the kitchen. Remember, you're sharing a common reality with the other people in the room, so you can always talk about what's going on around you—the food, the speaker, the decor, the traffic, or the activities of the group. At the very least, make sure to read your local paper the morning of the event. You'll be up on current events, local crime statistics, and other news in your town, which is always good for a conversation.

"I Have Nothing to Wear"

Clothing can be a real obstacle if your budget is tight. But that just makes for more interesting solutions:

1. Borrow clothes from a friend.
2. Invest in one good outfit and wear it again and again. For women, one great ensemble with rotating accessories goes a long way. Men can get a lot of mileage out of one good suit with rotating ties and shirts. Formal wear can be rented. Nobody will ever know.
3. Become an expert in shopping sales and discount stores. Figure out exactly what you need and resolve to buy only that item. Look in the newspaper for department store and discount store sales, and build a wardrobe for very little money. Nowhere is it written that good clothes have to be expensive.

"I Don't Know Where to Go"

In every city or town, local newspapers list events of all types—community, political, entertainment, charitable, educational, and business-oriented. In most large cities you can find monthly or weekly business journals and magazines on the newsstand that list lectures, awards banquets, seminars, and a variety of other events. The Sunday entertainment sections of daily newspapers are also loaded with events. You can also contact your Chamber of Commerce for information about its many social gatherings.

Get involved in the trade associations affiliated with the business you're in (or the business you'd like to be in), and read the trade publications for information on meetings, dinners, and other get-togethers. Join political action groups that attract the kinds of people you want to meet (and support causes you believe in). The Convention and Visitors Bureaus (CVBs) of most cities publish directories and events listings that cover a wide range of interests. For more suggestions, see the Resource List at the back of this book.

Are you getting the idea? There are very few excuses that can really hold water. The only acceptable reason for not going out there and *doing something* is that you aren't truly interested in networking and expanding your circle of friends and associates. And that's perfectly fine. Which brings us to the world-class all-time award winner.

"I Don't Have Time"

Isn't that a beauty? The clean delivery? The easy execution? The way it rolls off your tongue? That's why it's everyone's favorite.

The time issue is a big one, and it's a true perennial because it's so easy to use. Not only will people not argue with you when you cop out this way, they're probably going to respect you for being such a busy—and clearly, important—person.

But remember that conspicuous busy-ness is out of style in the 1990s. The Yuppies of the 1980s who worked 75-hour weeks to buy BMWs are a little older, wiser, and more tired now, and have learned to value "nonproductive" things like spending time at home with their children.

Your time *is* your own. Regardless of job or lifestyle demands, you have the final say about how you spend your time, and if someone in your life is telling you otherwise, you might consider making some changes and taking charge. Everybody is free to determine his or her own priorities, and if coming home from work and having dinner every night with the family at 6:30 is important to you, then that should be one of yours. That's how you choose to spend your time. You can also choose to spend those same hours one night per week Power Schmoozing *if going out into the world is important to you as well.* The choice is yours. There's no judgment here about what is right or wrong. It's completely up to you. It's your life. You get to make it up as you go along.

The next time you really want to do something like going to a lecture, or learning to speak Italian, or starting an exercise program, *but you don't have time,* try taking more responsibility for having made that choice. Instead of saying, "I don't have time," try saying, "Exercising is just not a big priority for me right now. I'd rather sleep late in the mornings." Because that would be the truth. And once you make a commitment to your own personal truth, you can't complain about the fact that you're not exercising. You've taken responsibility for your choice.

When exercise (or wine tasting, or Power Schmoozing) really does become important to you, the time will miraculously make itself available.

Other Common Problems in Social Interacting

In addition to the excuses mentioned above, there are some universal problems that plague us all. Here's a breakdown of some of the problems that students in my seminars mention on a regular basis:

1. Being Perceived as a Sex Object When You Don't Want to Be

First and foremost, be honest. Are you sure that you really don't want to be? If you're single, and in the back of your mind you're really hoping to meet someone special at the annual meeting of the National Association of Dental Hygienists, then don't be surprised if it shows. People are a lot more perceptive than we usually give them credit for, and if you combine that with the fact that your intentions are often louder than your words, people are going to naturally come on to you if you're in the market for a mate.

Have you ever noticed that when you're happily mated in a committed relationship, nobody tries to hit on you? Why is this? Because when you're truly unavailable, it shows, and acts as a barrier against unwanted intruders. For more on this, see Chapter 8.

2. Interacting with People from Other Cultures

The key word here is respect. You must always respect other peoples' cultural differences, even when you're not trying to impress them. A few years ago, I interviewed a Japanese architect for a magazine article. We met in a restaurant, and when we walked through the door that led from the foyer to the dining area, he practically shoved me out of the way so he could enter the room first.

It was quite embarrassing for both of us, since I was accustomed to men waiting for me to walk through a door first, and his actions really took me by surprise. I was aware that this was an old Japanese custom (I just didn't think modern businesspeople practiced it!), so I put on my humble hat and played the submissive female for the rest of the meeting.

Always take a moment to become familiar with etiquette and behavior codes if you're going to be working or socializing with people from other cultures.

3. Who Pays?

In business, it's generally assumed that the person who suggests the lunch is, in an indirect way, offering to pick up the tab. But this is not always the case. In a business situation where one person is "pitching" another, the person doing the pitching probably ought to pay the bill. After all, this is a seduction scenario, and if you're trying to win someone's business, you should plan on paying for the meal. However, if the other person reaches for the bill before you do, let her do it. It's embarrassing—not noble—to fight over who has the honor of paying. If it's a job interview, the potential employer should pay. After all, he has a job and you don't.

In more casual situations, you can simply ask your companion when the check arrives, "Shall we split this?" Many people don't know that you can give a waiter two credit cards and he or she will divide the tab equally between both. Don't be embarrassed to ask. Waiters do it all the time, and they're used to it.

Finally, if you feel that it is your companion who should be paying, simply ignore the bill when it arrives. That increases the odds of your partner acting on his or her own. It's been said that the longer the bill sits on the table, the louder it screams.

4. Talking to Someone Who Has Bad Breath

Always carry breath mints or gum with you. When you come face to face with this situation, take them out and pop one into *your* mouth, and then offer one to the offending person. If he refuses, smile and say, "Are you sure?" Then let it go.

5. To Drink or Not to Drink?

Trust your intuition on this one. At lunch meetings where you're trying to impress someone you don't know very well, it might be wise not to order wine or a cocktail unless your companion does. You don't want his or her judgment to be swayed by your imbibing. However, if you're living a life in which you're allowed to be yourself at all times, and you really want a glass of wine with lunch, then by all means, order one. You don't want to set yourself up in a new relationship where you're expected to be something that you're not. The same is true if you're dining with recovering alcoholics. Part of what they've learned in recovery is how to live in a world where other people drink. It's not your responsibility to shield them from temptation.

At dinner of course, it's more acceptable to drink, unless your partner happens to be someone whose personal or religious beliefs are strongly antialcohol. In that case, if your goal is to appear socially and/or morally aligned with this person, the obvious choice is to abstain. However, if you're a drinker (and a freethinker) and your prospective new client is a Mormon, then you might want to reconsider the project.

6. Talking to Celebrities

Celebrities are accustomed to being harassed, worshipped, gossiped about, stared at, intruded upon, and a number of other horrors. The best thing you can do around them is to respect them as you would anyone else. The worst thing you can do is make the gap between them and you even more apparent than it already is.

If you're at a social function and you spot a celebrity whom you've always wanted to meet, what do you do? A lot of it depends on what you want from him. If you just want to say hello and tell him how much you admire his work, then simply approach him and say just that. Then exit quickly. Don't hang around just for the sake of hanging around. If you have something else in mind—like asking him to perform at a benefit for your nonprofit group—introduce yourself, and ask him who among his representatives you might contact to ask for his participation.

If he's interested in you and your project (and he has a few minutes to talk to you), he may ask for details right then and there, but give him the shortest, most concise pitch humanly possible. If he's not interested, let him give you the name of his publicist or manager, and be satisfied with that. It's very rude to pitch someone directly in a social setting. For more on this subject, see Chapter 13.

7. Introductions

Always introduce the person you are with to anyone new who approaches. It's terribly rude to leave someone standing there while you break off the conversation to say hello to a new person. Making an introduction helps include the first person in the conversation.

An important issue that comes up concerning introducing people is whether or not to define the person by his or her job description. For instance, at a party, would you introduce Jill, an IRS auditor, to Angela, a CPA, by saying, "This is Jill Benson—she's an auditor for the IRS"? Of course you would! It's traditionally done this way at business-oriented functions to promote networking and deal making. As the person who's acting as host-for-the-moment, it's your job to connect these two people, and by giving them a little more information about each other, you've helped to make their conversation that much easier.

But what if Jill and Angela were also both mothers at your 3-year-old son's birthday party? Or you and Angela, while out shopping together, ran into Jill at the mall? Would their careers be relevant in this context? I still say yes. A person's career and interests are an intrinsic part of who he or she is, and by giving people an identifying "tag" during a introduction, you're giving them a common bond that can get them started on an interesting conversation, or potentially lead to a mutually rewarding long-term relationship.

And that's a nice thing to do for a friend.

How to Host a Successful Party or Event

One of the most effective ways to keep in touch with the new people you're meeting is to invite them to parties. If the people you're targeting are inaccessible or unresponsive to your calls or letters, giving them an opportunity to get out and do some of their own networking will appeal to their opportunistic instincts. If they're productive, interesting people, they'll want to expand their circle of friends and associates as much as you do.

In the business world, inviting someone you're hoping to impress to a memorable party at your home can make a big difference in the type of relationship you create with that person. Remember that the goal is not just to get your foot in someone's door so that he'll become your client or give you a job: the goal is to make a friend, acquaintance, or an ally. If the relationship begins on equal ground, where you're two peers socializing together, the effects generated by that relationship will be wider reaching and longer lasting.

Let's say you've had the good fortune to meet Ron—an influential person in your industry—at a trade show, a party, or a business meeting with other colleagues. You had a stimulating conversation, and you genuinely liked him. When the encounter was over (which may have lasted a few minutes or a few hours), you exchanged business cards with the unspoken acknowledgment of your mutual interest in each other, and went your separate ways.

This is typical of the majority of first social encounters in the business world. If it had been an encounter between two people who had a sexual interest in each other, the next step would be obvious: One would ask the other for a date and the intentions would be understood. But in a nonsexual situation, it might seem a little odd to ask Ron if he was free for dinner Tuesday night. It would be perfectly acceptable, however, and put a lot less pressure on Ron, if you invited him to join you at a party you're throwing on your boat next weekend. To play it even safer, you could simply add Ron's address to your database and make sure to invite him to your next get-together.

I recently worked with a photographer on a project for one of my clients. It turned out that she had a daughter the same age as my son, and her husband was a writer for a major publication. We had a great time joking around together during the photo session. She was someone I wanted to keep track of for two reasons: I liked her very much on a personal level and considered her a potential friend and she had outstanding media connections, which could benefit me professionally. But she and I didn't know each other well enough to meet for lunch any time soon or get together with our husbands and children at the park. So instead, I invited her and her family to a barbecue I was planning for a group of my friends and their kids. It was an opportunity to get to know her better in a casual environment with very little pressure, surrounded by other people with whom she'd have something in common.

Let's say that Ron, from our earlier example, is a buyer for a large department store and you're a clothing designer. You live in a small apartment, hate cooking, and never have parties, but you're a member of a fashion industry trade group which has its annual Christmas party coming up. Ron is in the fashion industry, and may even know some of the people who will be there, so why not invite him to the event? You don't have to invite him as your guest, which may be too presumptuous at this early stage of the game, but you can casually mention the event and ask if he'd like to drop by. You can double the impact by following up with a letter containing the announcement or tickets to the event.

Inviting new contacts to parties and other social events is a great way to reveal something of yourself to your prospects. It's another way of telling your whole story, and an opportunity to spend more time with new people in a relaxed setting that encourages candor.

Planning great parties is an art that requires skill, experience, and finesse, and very few people are truly good at it. Not everyone enjoys entertaining and being the center of attention. But you don't have to be the slickest host in town with a flair for fabulous buffets and glamorous guests lists to pull it off. You just have to be bold and creative. If you hate socializing, have a small home, a limited budget, and a wallflower personality, you can still throw a great party by enlisting the help of friends.

The How and Why of Parties

I recently met a man who was famous for his political activities in the 1960s. He had just moved to Los Angeles from New York, where he'd organized a series of popular networking events, but in L.A. he didn't know many people. He'd heard about my seminars, and called me to introduce himself, thinking that we'd have some common interests. We met and really hit it off, and agreed to exchange contacts by taking each other to parties and events we'd been invited to.

His first offering to me was to get me on the guest list for an exclusive political fund-raiser where a lot of powerful people would be gathered. My first offering to him was to invite him to my annual New Year's Day party, which would be attended by dozens of people who knew his reputation and would love to meet him.

In another example, a friend of mine named Maggie—a marketing director for a large Los Angeles hospital—was unexpectedly fired when the hospital was bought by an international megacorporation. Maggie knew that I worked as a marketing consultant for several area hospitals, so she called me to see if I knew of any leads she could pursue for a new job. I knew of nothing offhand, but I was scheduled to meet Carol, the chief financial officer of a major hospital, to discuss an unrelated project the next day, and I promised Maggie I'd ask if there were any positions available.

The meeting with Carol went very well. We liked each other immediately, and exchanged life stories over lunch. I told her that Maggie was looking for a job, and she said that Maggie could contact the personnel director, Mr. Jackson, who would have some openings in mid-January. I ended up inviting Carol to the same New Year's Day party to which I'd invited the 1960s radical (I like an eclectic mix of people at my parties). Maggie was also invited, of course, and when I returned to my office I called Maggie to tell her that Carol would be there, and that she should try to get to know her a bit during the party, so that when she sent her résumé to Mr. Jackson, she could say that Carol referred her. Sounds a bit convoluted, but that's how it works. A party planner should also function as a matchmaker.

Bringing people together is the primary function of parties. They're like showcases—a stage for introducing new faces, bringing new people into the fold, launching new relationships, and building new families. Parties can happen anywhere, any time, for any reason, at homes, offices, restaurants, or public parks. They can be casual backyard get-togethers with neighbors, children, and dogs, or black-tie affairs in hotel ballrooms. Powerful, important people go to children's birthday parties and family picnics just like the rest of us, so don't think you have to rent the Ritz to make your party a success. There are, however, some very definite rules for designing successful parties, which, if followed, work magically for everything from a formal wedding for 500 to a keg party in a parking lot.

How to Work Your Own Party

Your own party is the easiest to work because you're on your own turf with your own friends, and you're in complete control. The biggest mistake most people make is that they feel it would be too aggressive and pushy to actually use that control, so they tend to leave their guests to fend for themselves, which can make for very bored guests. Many of us envision a successful party as one in which a room full of attractive people laugh and mingle and eat and drink among themselves, with nice music in the background or maybe even a live band. After all, we're adults. We're capable of meeting others unassisted, having stimulating conversations, and keeping ourselves amused and entertained. Right?

Wrong! If you think about all the parties you've attended, you'll see that after a while you got weary of struggling to meet people, of constantly saying, "Hi. Are you a friend of the bride or the groom? Nice earrings. What business are you in?" And if the music was loud, this exercise became truly pointless, because no one could hear a word you were saying, and your throat hurt from shouting. You probably left the party feeling unfulfilled, because you never really managed to have a good conversation with anyone.

Let's look at some examples.

I recently attended a very elaborate party, which was essentially a formal, black-tie "barn dance" for just over 100 people. The hostess was celebrating her fortieth birthday, and had the good fortune to be both wealthy and generous, so she spared no expense in making the event memorable. She invited everyone—childhood friends, old boyfriends, college buddies, and family members—and she paid the airfare for out-of-towners, and put all of us up in first-class hotels. She hired the best caterer in the state, and had the barn on her rural property professionally decorated—complete with chandeliers and a temporary dance floor! She had her favorite musical group flown in from her home state, and even had the barn rewired so it could handle the electrical load generated by the band's equipment.

The party began at 7 p.m., and everyone arrived in formal attire. The champagne poured freely, the hors d'oeuvres were wonderful, and the band was hot. People ate, danced, and mingled excitedly, and by all appearances, this promised to be a rollicking bash. But as the hours wore on with the energy driving at a constant, boisterous high, something began to happen. People started to slow down and, dare I say, became bored. At 9 p.m., the dinner was ready (it wasn't announced— people just started figuring it out and eventually drifted toward the buffet area). During dinner, the energy in the room remained at the same intense pitch. Some people ate while others continued to frolic, and the band kept playing loudly, which made dinner conversation nearly impossible.

Another hour passed this way with more of the same: return trips to the bar, a dance or two, maybe a new face to shout at over the loud amplified music. We'd now been reveling freely for 3 hours, without the slightest alteration in the energy level, or sound level, or any shift in the focus of our attention.

By 11 p.m., everyone was quite drunk, drinking more and more in an attempt to keep the party spirit alive. The plan was for the band to make a big birthday presentation at midnight, with a three-tiered cake, a cascade of balloons, a champagne toast, and a special dance for the birthday girl and her husband. But by the time midnight arrived, we had been there for 5 hours *with no leadership,* and spirits were sagging.

Leadership. Not exactly a word one tends to associate with lively parties. But contrary to what many of us believe, leadership is desperately needed at most parties, and can make the difference between a great party and a dull one. The black-tie barn dance was successful. Everyone had a good time, or seemed to, even though in 5 long hours, not once did our hostess or any of her admirers step up to the microphone to welcome us, lead us in a toast, announce that dinner was served, or *provide us with anything to do.* We were left on our own to amuse ourselves, and to find people to talk with, and over such a long period of time, against a backdrop of loud music and lots of alcohol, it became hard work. The lesson here is that *a host should never make guests work hard at amusing themselves.*

The reason games like "Pin the Tail on the Donkey" are played at children's birthday parties is that kids have short attention spans. They get bored just playing on their own.

Adults are like children in this way, only our play is different—we eat and drink, flirt and schmooze. But that gets boring too. We need to have variations in the focus and energy levels at parties in order to keep them interesting.

If I decided to host a black-tie barn dance, here's what I'd do to keep my guests happy:

1. After giving the guests 30 or 45 minutes to settle in, have a drink or two, and schmooze a little, I'd step onto the stage and welcome them, maybe giving them a short rundown on what the evening's agenda would entail, and thank a few of the people who helped put the event together. Then I would introduce the band. (If you're not good at speaking to crowds, you can appoint an outgoing friend to act as "emcee" for your party. Outgoing types love this job.)

2. After the band's first set (about 45 to 60 minutes), I'd return to the stage to announce that the buffet was now being served. I'd have the band play different music for dinner, something more conducive to conversation. This would create a shift in the energy, an opportunity for people to actually talk to one another.

3. During dinner, I might arrange some humorous entertainment: a tribute to the guest of honor, or testimonials from friends fondly reminiscing about their younger years together. Maybe a particular friend had prepared something special, like a song or silly award, or some comical memento from the guest of honor's life. After this, the band could resume, dancing would take up again, and guests could be left to their own devices until it was time for the birthday cake and the big finale.

The idea here is to help the flow move along by shaping and shifting people's attention. A simple change in music or lighting during dinner can completely transform a room. And people need that! The last time I enjoyed a party filled with 5 hours of intensely loud music and no structure was when I was in my twenties and too stoned to care.

Party Games

I once hosted a wedding shower for a friend. There were about 50 people in my house, most of whom I'd never met before. Being the irreverent extrovert that I am, I decided to make the party fun by organizing a game, for which I would gather everyone together after the party had been going for about an hour. It was a home version of the old TV show *The Newlywed Game*, and I had devised personalized questions for the bride and groom, sequestering one in another room while the other answered, just like on TV. It was a riot, and everyone loved it.

At a baby shower for my former husband and me when our son was born, the hostess organized a game that provided us with beautiful memories to last our family forever. She called the room to order after lunch had been served, and passed out sheets of paper and pencils. Each guest had to write a little story about what kind of life they predicted our newborn son would have in 30 years, and then read their stories to the group. The results ran the gamut from poignant and sincere to hysterically funny, and included everything from a wilderness explorer who discovers an herbal cure for cancer in an Andean weed patch, to a Wall Street corporate raider who wrests control of his father's business in a hostile takeover. I keep all these stories in a scrapbook, and can't wait until the day when we can all sit down and read them together 25 years from now.

There are many simple networking games for large groups that are very effective in encouraging people to mingle. For instance, try asking guests to form a circle and take turns telling a little bit about who they are and what they're interested in. You'll be amazed at how people will enjoy being the center of attention, if only for a minute or two. When this is over and the circle breaks, everyone will have chosen someone to meet on the basis of what was said in the circle, and the conversation in the room will suddenly become more animated, more relaxed, and more productive.

At a recent dinner party for about 8 people, we played a silly and simple game called "Celebrity," which contributed a lot to the evening's success. Each person writes the names of

10 famous people on 10 separate strips of paper. All the strips get thrown into a bowl, and the players then pair off. One person in the pair picks a name from the bowl, and attempts to get his or her partner to guess who the celebrity is by giving hints (such as the name of the celeb's last movie, the latest gossip about him, or her position in politics) without giving away the name. Names can be sports figures, movie stars, political leaders, or any famous individuals. You can make up your own rules.

The point of all this is that we need to have our attention guided and manipulated sometimes. Having a central focus in a room full of people helps unite everybody in common thought. It reaffirms our reason for being there. It entertains us and loosens us up, and helps develop our sense of belonging.

The idea of having an "emcee" for a party may seem a bit controlling, but don't knock it till you've tried it. Look at what bar mitzvah and wedding bandleaders do. What would these events be like if they didn't invite the bar mitzvah boy's family to the stage to light the candles, or if the bride and groom didn't steal the show with their romantic first dance as a married couple?

If you have a friend who's got a funny, outgoing personality and loves to perform (and we all know someone like that), ask him or her to emcee your next party (or your wedding), and see what happens. (For more details about parties, see my book *When Good People Throw Bad Parties: A Guide to Party Politics for Hosts and Guests*, published by First House Press.)

*   *   *   *   *

What Works at Parties

- An agenda, games, a program, activities, and/or an emcee
- Keeping boisterous pets outside or in another room
- A balance of sensible and extravagant foods
- Assigning tasks to guests who ask for them (*it makes them feel useful, especially for very shy guests*)

- Something for kids to do (*in a safe space, preferably separate from the adults*)
- Keeping the music in the background (*if you want conversation*)
- Introducing people by giving more information than simply their names (*"Ray, this is Angela. She just arrived from Atlanta. Angela, Ray's son lives in Atlanta."*)
- A comfortable space (*lighting, seating, temperature, sound level*)
- Hired help for serving, cleaning, or child care, so that the host can have fun too

*   *   *   *   *

*   *   *   *   *

What Doesn't Work at Parties

- Throwing a group of people together with no focus, agenda, or purpose, and expecting them to fend for themselves
- Poorly chosen food (*serving only junk food or solely meat-based dishes will alienate at least half your guests*)
- Not enough food
- Extremely loud music that forces people to shout in order to be heard (*unless you're all under 25*)
- An uncomfortable space (*too large, too small, too cold, too hot, too bright, too dark*)
- Odd hours (*holding a wine-tasting party in your downtown office at 4 p.m. on a weekday when your guests have to drive home in rush-hour traffic—drunk*)
- Stringent themes that harshly impose on people's identities (*avoid asking people to dress as their favorite vegetable*)
- Filling the room with too many people of the same type (*don't invite only golf-playing doctors; mix and match social stratas, ages, professions, and political affinities*)

*   *   *   *   *

Talking to Celebrities

Here's a stunning visual image for you. At this moment I'm sitting in the empty bleachers of the 12,000-seat Garden Arena of the MGM Grand Hotel in Las Vegas. I'm here at an afternoon rehearsal for a star-studded benefit concert that will take place in about 6 hours, and singer Michael Bolton is standing 15 feet in front of me talking with record producer David Foster. Country music superstar Wynonna Judd is 8 feet to my left, and I've just finished having a conversation with Robin Williams about how much we hate Las Vegas (he said, "Even Fellini would find this place too weird"). Tonight I'll be sitting at a table with artist Peter Max, adjacent to other tables where Elton John, attorney Robert Shapiro, and tennis star Andre Agassi will be seated. It's an interesting mix of the rich and famous, and includes actors, musicians, political figures, and sports stars. Something for everybody.

I'm here because my husband, Michael, is a photographer who specializes in shooting events like this, and he's asked me to assist him this weekend. It's been an intense education in celebrity protocol, and that's why I decided to pull out my laptop computer and write this chapter while I'm sitting here at the rehearsal. Michael is the definitive expert on the subject, having photographed just about every major celebrity on the planet. I defer to him on all matters concerning how to act around the rich and famous, and when I go with him to the Academy Awards or other glitzy gatherings, I feel like I'm studying with the Master.

Not that I'm completely without my own experience in this realm. In the early 1980s I worked as an assistant to Rick Springfield, who was a Grammy-winning rock star at the time. I traveled with him on occasion, and everywhere we went he was mobbed by hormonal teenage girls. It was fun for him at first, but it got old fast. He spent a lot of time being depressed on the road. They all do. It's an occupational hazard. Ever since then, when I see a famous person making his or her way through a public place, I'm overwhelmed by sadness. It's very difficult for them. It's a weird way to live. But it's also part of the job description, and that's the trade-off they make for the big bucks and the ego strokes. The first thing you need to know if you're serious about learning how to talk to celebrities, is to learn a little about how life looks *to them*.

Yesterday, here in Las Vegas, Michael and I were walking toward the hotel elevator and Robin Williams, having just arrived at the hotel, was walking in front of us. Even though he had the gait of someone trying to hide—stooped shoulders, head down, eyes averted—he was stopped every couple of seconds by someone asking for his autograph. Remarkably, he made it to the elevator, and we got in after him. There was one other person in there with us, a man with a baby in a stroller. Robin pushed the button for his floor, and I said to him, "You're a brave man walking through the casino alone like that." He said, "It's easier that way."

Then we arrived at our floor, said good-bye, and got out. The man with the baby got out behind us, and a group of his friends were there waiting for him. As we started down the hallway, we heard the guy say to his friends, "That was Robin Williams in the elevator!" The whole group shrieked in unison and pushed madly on the elevator button, trying to bring Robin back. Fortunately, Robin escaped in the nick of time. Later that night, at the preconcert reception, Robin arrived with his wife and was immediately surrounded by admirers. The wife disappeared into the background while Robin commenced to do an important part of his job—schmoozing with his public (at least the ones who were lucky enough to get invited to the reception). One awestruck person after another came up to say hello and bask in Robin's light for a few moments. Because this was a high-ticket fund-raiser for a charity, the people in the room had lots of money, and at least two of them offered to donate $500 to the charity if Robin would pose for a photo with them. Others simply asked him to pose with them without offering a donation, and he gladly agreed. He was receptive and professional. He welcomed them all with warmth and respect.

There are two points of view when it comes to talking to celebrities: yours and theirs. For them, being nice to you is part of their job, and most of them willingly accept this responsibility. In fact, many are actually quite accessible and friendly. Others can be shut down, angry, defensive, and obnoxious. The distribution of these behaviors in the celebrity world is about the same as it is in the rest of world—it's random, and you never know what you're going to get. This applies to all kinds of VIPs, whether it's the mayor of a small town, the chairman of a megacorporation, or a glamorous movie star. And the rules that govern how best to interact with them apply across the board, whether you're in Hollywood, California, or Cottonwood, Nebraska.

Giving and Taking

My grandmother, who passed away in 1990, had been in an intimate relationship with one of Milton Berle's brothers for 10 years. When she was in the hospital, Milton came to see her, and I ran into him in the hospital lobby when we were both on our way up to her room. We took the elevator together, talking about Grandma's condition.

As we walked through the crowded hospital corridors, dozens of people approached him, filled with love and adoration, saying things like, "Oh, it's Milton Berle! I've loved you for 30 years, I'm so happy to meet you! But what are doing here at the hospital? I hope there's nothing wrong with your health, God forbid!" Milton was quite the gentleman, smiling and reassuring them that his health was just fine, signing autographs and cracking jokes. It was heartwarming to see the love radiating from his fans.

When we got to Grandma's room, we joined the relatives who had gathered there, including one very distant uncle Sid, whom I hadn't seen since I was 4 years old. We all talked to Grandma, trying to make her feel good, except for Sid, who did nothing but suck up to Milton by saying things like, "My cousin in Buffalo met you back in 1961 at the racetrack. His name was Arnold Rosen. Do ya remember him?"

It was embarrassing for all of us, and it hit an all-time tasteless low when Sid finally blurted out something about wanting Milton to perform for the Jewish Welfare League's upcoming charity bash, for which Sid was apparently some kind of chairperson.

Very tacky. And unfortunate, because Sid's charity was probably quite worthwhile. I have nothing against pitching celebrities to help with worthy causes, but Sid's approach was the ultimate in bad taste and ignorance. Milton responded by telling Sid to contact his manager, but even if Sid had followed up in this way, Milton would have had a bad first impression of Sid, and the chance of his agreeing to appear would be greatly decreased.

There was a very big difference between the way Sid acted and the way the other people in the hospital corridors did. The other people were *giving* something to Milton, showing their love and their concern for his health. Sid was only *taking*.

Let's go back to Robin Williams in the elevator. My comment to him about being brave was a gentle, compassionate piece of recognition. I asked for nothing in return. The screaming people who pushed the elevator button were *takers* (he would have had very little respect for them if the elevator car had deposited him back at their floor). On the other hand, the people at the charity reception were *givers*. There was an *exchange* of energy going on there. They were contributing either their time or their money to the cause, just like Robin was. And that made them equals. I'm not saying you need to throw money around in order to connect with famous people. But when talking to them, you need to focus on giving rather than taking.

As a great example of giving, I saw a man in line at the supermarket one day who realized that Martin Landau was in line ahead of him. After Landau paid for his groceries and turned to leave, the man quietly called after him and said, "Mr. Landau, you should have won an Oscar for *Crimes and Misdemeanors.*" Landau's face lit up, he smiled, said, "Thank you," and went on his way.

It was a fair exchange. The fan gave something to the star. When I tell this story in my seminars, I'm always asked, "But fans give to stars all the time by seeing their movies or buying their products. Can't a fan expect something in return?" When I posed this question to Michael, his answer was, "The stars *already* gave." And I agree completely. All you have to do is look closely at one of them the next time you see him slinking through a hotel lobby trying to hide his face.

Fan Behavior vs. Professional Behavior

There are two types of encounters you can have with a celebrity. One type occurs between a star and a fan. The other is reserved for people who need to meet celebs because it will help further their career goals. Let's start by looking at fan behavior.

We're drawn to famous people, particularly performers, because they carry our projections for us. They literally act our feelings for us, and on top of that, they're usually beautiful and rich. When we meet them, we want to absorb some of their powerful energy. We feel intimate with them because we've observed them doing things on screen or on stage that we rarely witness people doing in real life. We've seen actors in movies have sex, give birth, battle the elements, kill someone, and be killed (how many times have you watched your friends or neighbors doing these things?). These are intense images, and even though we're smart enough to know that it's all fantasy, we still connect the actor with the experience.

If you feel that you absolutely must comment to celebrities about how great they are and how much you love them, then follow the example of the man at the market. Give the celebrity your compliment, and then *let go*. Celebs enjoy being recognized and acknowledged (who doesn't?), but they don't enjoy being harassed, and unfortunately many of us unwittingly make them uncomfortable because we have a burning need to connect with them. How would you feel if everyone who saw you wanted to stop and chat? It would drive you crazy.

Instead, next time you're waiting for your car at the car wash and you find yourself sitting on the bench next to Bruce Willis, try acting normal. He knows he's Bruce Willis. You know he's Bruce Willis. Is it really necessary to point it out? If you feel you just have to talk to him, talk about the reality you're sharing at the moment. "So how do you like your BMW? I hear it did well in the *Consumer Reports* crash test," might be a good opening line. This way, you can walk away feeling like you didn't make a fool of yourself, you approached him as an equal (two people having their cars washed), and you can tell everyone you had a conversation with a star.

Choose your subject matter carefully. My ex-husband, Jim, who owns a recording studio that does sound for television and film, once talked with Gregory Peck in the studio lounge. Mr. Peck was relaxing between takes of a recording for an American history project. This inspired Jim to start talking passionately about a left-wing political idea he believed in, and the ignorance of its detractors. The only trouble was that Peck had recently chaired a staunchly conservative organization opposed to Jim's way of thinking *on that very issue*. And although Jim wasn't being personally offensive, he was unaware of the star's affiliation, and managed to make the dignified Mr. Peck a very uncomfortable client in his own studio.

In Los Angeles, New York, and other big cities, superstars can be spotted in restaurants, airports, and other public places. It also happens in small towns, where a production company might be shooting a movie, or a celebrity might be visiting family or taking a vacation. One afternoon while I was having lunch with a friend in a small health-food restaurant, Magic Johnson walked in. Now here's a man who's impossible to miss when he walks into a room by virtue of his size as well as his celebrity. Even though a lot of us here in L.A. are pretty jaded when it comes to seeing stars, the moment Magic walked in, everybody in the place was stunned and the room went silent for a few seconds while all heads turned to look at him. But just as quickly, we all pulled ourselves together and went back to the business of eating and talking, stealing a glance at him whenever we could do so without being intrusive. Nobody approached him to ask for his autograph or inquire about his health. Nobody asked him for anything. We just left him alone, which was the most respectful thing we could do.

A similar incident occurred later that same week, when I was having dinner with my father in a French restaurant. Johnny Carson was seated in the booth next to us. Nobody even looked twice. To approach a celebrity while he's eating is extremely bad manners. An alternative might be to time your exit so that it coincides with his, and approach him in the parking lot. "Hi, Johnny. How ya doing?" would be the proper thing to say. Nothing more. If you have a camera with you and you want a picture with him, it's OK to ask. That's what fans are expected to do. But shoot the picture, say thank you, and then get out of there.

If you want to schmooze with stars, corporate bigwigs, or politicians to help your career, there are two different approaches you can take. One is to give a blatantly aggressive pitch on yourself and your talents, and the other is to carefully cultivate a long-term, meaningful relationship.

In the first scenario, you happen upon an influential person and you boldly thrust your résumé, product sample, screenplay, or brochure into the guy's face. He immediately falls in love with the product/screenplay/résumé, and offers you a high-paying, glamorous position with a guaranteed future, on the spot. Of course it's a fantasy to think you can win someone's attention and respect this way, but strangely enough, it has been known to happen in rare circumstances.

Bill, a musician friend of mine in the early 1980s, had a day job as a sandwich vendor selling door-to-door in office buildings. He always carried a cassette tape of his band's music with him, because many of the offices housed record companies, and Bill was hoping for a chance to get his tape into the right hands. His big break arrived when he spotted one of the record industry's top producers at the time, Ted Templeman, walking across the parking lot toward his car. He dashed across the lot and got there just as Ted was getting into his Porsche. Bill pulled out his tape, rapid-fired an explanation of the band and its music, and *begged* Ted to listen to it. Ted shrugged, took the tape, said he'd listen in the car, and drove away. Later that same day, Bill got a call from Ted's record company asking him to come in for a meeting. Within a year, Bill's band was working on its second album.

This kind of thing really does happen, but the odds are highly stacked against it, and you'd need an absolutely perfect-at-that-particular-moment product to get the kind of response my friend got. Feel free to try it, though. But remember, if your goal is to be perceived as an equal instead of a needy person desperate for a career break, then this approach would be inappropriate for you. In that case, there's another method, which can be effective over the long term, but rarely offers immediate gratification. It's called "going through the back door." This is the long-term-cultivation-of-a-relationship approach.

The idea here is to establish relationships with famous people by making contact with them through the *back door,* which means bypassing the normal channels (sending letters via agents and managers or leaving phone messages with secretaries). The way to do this is to get involved in the activities in which *they're* involved, like political causes, charities, children's activities, and other projects. If you get in deeply enough, you'll start seeing the same people again and again. You'll start working with them. You'll meet their friends. And your network of contacts and acquaintances will expand to include them.

There was a young, handsome actor named Carl in one of my seminars who was desperate to connect with casting agents and directors. He spent his days sending his photos around, going to open-casting calls, and doing the usual pavement pounding that aspiring actors do. One Saturday afternoon, his brother Ed took him along to help out at a bake sale at Ed's daughter's elementary school in Beverly Hills. Carl didn't exactly relish the idea of spending a whole day with a bunch of kids. "After all," he figured, "what's a cool guy like me going to gain by going to some dumb bake sale?"

But to his amazement, Carl found himself working next to one of the casting agents he'd been trying to reach for weeks. It turned out that the agent's daughter went to the same school, and there this powerful woman was, bagging oatmeal cookies with Carl. He had a long, friendly conversation with her, and through his newly formed relationship with his niece and the school, he had created the possibility of future contact with the agent. What an opportunity!

But that's all it is. An opportunity. Chatting it up with an agent at a bake sale (or with an industry tycoon on the golf course) isn't enough to help you get your "big break." It's only the beginning. You have to work very hard at cultivating that relationship, even though it might not "pay off" for a couple of years.

In Carl's example, there are several ways he can go about it. He can get involved with the school, perhaps volunteering to be a reading tutor or carpool driver. If the agent's daughter is doing poorly in math (Carl might have learned this in their conversation), he could volunteer to tutor her once a week. Or maybe during their initial conversation Carl learned that the agent takes her daughter to a particular playground in the neighborhood. Carl can start taking his niece there on a regular basis, and hope that he'll run into her again. If that happened, the two kids might play together, the agent would remember Carl from the bake sale, and they could all become friends.

It's a lot of work. There's a definite art to it, and patience plays a big part. But that's how *all* friendships get started. Regardless of your intentions and reasons for wanting to schmooze with influential people, in the process, you're actually going to make new friends. The only difference is that the friends you're aiming for will probably be in a different social strata from the one you're in at the moment.

*　　*　　*　　*　　*

The Most Common Mistakes People Make When Talking to Celebrities

- *Putting the FP (Famous Person) on a Pedestal.* If you meet an FP at a party or event, and you're there as a guest, organizer, or participant, don't act like a fan. Act like an equal. Talk about what you have in common, such as the reason for the party you're both attending. Discuss politics, current events, the weather, the traffic, the meaning of life—whatever you'd talk to a "regular" person about. Remember, if you're in the same space at the same time as someone, you automatically have several things in common.

- *Clinging.* Once you've engaged an FP in a conversation, remember to *let go* when the conversation is over. Even though it would be great if you could hang out with him for a while, walk to the parking lot together, or buy him a drink, chances are you'll overstay your welcome if you try to make these things happen.

- *Name Dropping.* FPs won't be impressed with all the people you know unless you can show that you really have a personal, intimate relationship with someone *they* know. If you do mention someone you both know, then make sure it has some relevance to the conversation. Comments such as "I went to college with your cousin" are useless and embarrassing, and make you look like a loser. Instead, next time you're schmoozing with an FP at an event (such as a fund-raiser for charity), try this: "I'm really pleased that you're involved in this project. I've been working with Bob and Marcus (the organizers of the fund-raiser) for the last couple of years. They're doing a great job." *That's* relevant.

- *Pitching and Sucking Up.* Never, never ask an FP *out of context* to:

  Get involved in your favorite community project
  Look at your screenplay
  Coach your kid's little league team

In context, it's a different story. If you're meeting the FP for the purpose of working on a project together (let's say a fund-raiser for Pediatric AIDS), then in *that* context, you can tell her about related projects. If she's interested, she'll ask questions indicating her interest. If you've written a screenplay about children with AIDS, then it would be relevant to mention it.

The good news is that if you're on your way to see your doctor, and you find yourself in the medical building elevator next to Steven Spielberg, yes, you can pitch your screenplay, if you happen to have it in your hand at the time. You'll probably never see the guy again, so what have you got to lose by shoving it into his face? It's different if you're trying to build a relationship as an equal. But in a situation like an elevator, where there's little chance of a relationship evolving out of the brief encounter, by all means go for it.

- *Asking Too Many Questions.* If you're not a journalist conducting an interview, don't ask questions about the FP's latest movie, his divorce, or other career or personal info. You're not there to interview him. Remember, be an equal. Talk about the reality that the two of you *are sharing* at the moment.

- *Not Being Yourself.* Use your personality! The way to get the conversation beyond small talk is to charm the FP into "falling in love" with you, just as you would with anybody who interests you. If you chat for a minute about politics (especially if yours are in alignment with the FP's), then maybe your intellect, your wit, and your articulateness will impress her enough to steer the conversation toward your project, screenplay, acting abilities, or whatever else you hope to sell her on.

- *Screaming and Fawning and Acting Like an Idiot.* Does this really need an explanation?

*   *   *   *   *

Meeting the Rich, Famous, and Powerful on Their Own Turf

The story of Carl can have many variations. In my own life, I've gone through the back door by becoming involved in as many volunteer projects as I can handle. In earlier chapters I talked about how volunteering for tasks at parties and in organizations can make it easier to meet new people. In the world of celebrities, it can often be the *only* way.

If you become involved in a social cause with a large celebrity following, you can work your way up the ranks to the point where you'll be expected to attend formal social events where the rich and famous will be in attendance. The same is true for all kinds of organizations which attract celebrities, such as environmental groups, national and local charities, political groups, and arts associations. Do you know what wealthy honchos and stars do on Saturday nights? They go to $5000-a-plate fund-raising events for charities. If you're involved with one of these groups and attend its functions, you'll meet and get to know important people *through the back door.* In Los Angeles, where the power elite operates in an insulated little circle and everybody outside the circle wants to be on the inside, it's extremely difficult to break through. That's why I've been working with nonprofit groups for years. It was my ticket to the hippest parties in town.

For example, I'm a member of an organization that does a form of lobbying for environmental issues. I believe in the group so much that I volunteered to orchestrate a marketing campaign for it, to help increase its membership and spread the word about its work. As part of the marketing plan, with the help of other volunteers, we put on a benefit concert to raise money for the group.

It took months of planning, and during these months I contacted hundreds of VIPs by sending letters to them (through the front door) by way of their secretaries, managers, and other handlers. Many were familiar with the group and were interested in our work. Some wanted to participate in the concert, and some did not. But through my work on this project, I met—either in person or by phone—celebrities, their representatives, journalists, and other influential people whom I can now continue to build into my ever-expanding list of friends, associates, and contacts. When I met the celebrities at our fund-raising event, they perceived me as an involved, professional person whose political concerns paralleled their own. That made me an *equal*.

You don't have to be a marketing whiz to do this. You can volunteer whatever skills you have. My husband Michael began his career as a celebrity photographer by working for free—volunteering his services to nonprofit groups. Now, several years later, he gets paid as much as $2000 per day, but he'll still work for free on occasion for a social issue he believes in when there's not enough in the budget to pay him. He does this because he cares about the cause, but also because it's good networking. He also happens to be charming, unpretentious, and reliable, which is how he earned his reputation as a dependable guy as well as a great photographer. Almost all his work comes from referral. But nobody would know anything about him if he hadn't started out by volunteering and hanging out in the right places.

Even if all you can offer is help with stuffing envelopes or making phone calls, with a little commitment you can become a vital member of the team, and you will be included in the social events. At the back of this book is a list of national nonprofit organizations with regional chapters. They all need volunteers. And they all throw big parties which attract famous, powerful people.

That's how you meet them. Staying in touch with them is another story. In Chapter 10, I discussed many effective techniques for staying in touch with new people over long periods of time. These techniques work with celebrities just as well as with regular people. Once you've met them, once you've worked with them on a fund-raiser or other project, you can keep the communication alive by sending update letters on the progress of the organization (signed by you), invitations to other events, or newsletters. Eventually, after you've developed a credible relationship using the techniques in Chapter 10, the time will be right for you to pitch celebrities on *you*—as a writer, mechanic, chiropractor, housekeeper, architect, hairdresser, or therapist. Or as just an average person who has succeeded in making an impact on their lives—no matter who they are.

*   *   *   *   *

How to Make Friends with Celebrities

Do

- Follow every lead, no matter how insignificant it seems.
- Talk to people everywhere you go—the car wash, the park, the airport.
- Work for free—internships, special projects, community events.
- Volunteer *long term* for high-visibility nonprofit organizations.
- In conversations, give people information about yourself *other than* what you're doing or hope to do in the industry.
- Be conversationally assertive—introduce yourself to everyone in the room.
- Be socially assertive—host parties, organize projects and events, get involved.
- Offer your services in exchange for information and opportunities.
- Remember to go through the back door. These people have lives outside the office. Find them there.
- Stay informed about current events. Read the trades, but read everything else too.
- Use props and conversation pieces (kids, dogs, clothing) to get attention.

Don't

- Avoid social events because you think "no one important" will be there.

- Litter your conversation with the names of all the famous people you know because you think it will make *you* look important.
- Limit your conversations to shop talk.
- Cold-call schmooze targets and invite them to lunch in exchange for letting you sit at their feet and "pick their brains."
- Say "I'll do anything to get involved with your project." Desperation is unattractive.
- Lie. Ever. For any reason. Ever.
- Dress in costume (never be overtly trendy or blatantly sexual).
- Accept abuse just to get close to somebody.

*   *   *   *   *

Beyond Contacts...Friends

I remember my mother telling me when I was a teenager that making friends gets more difficult as you get older. Now that I'm older, I realize that she was only half right. It's not more difficult. It's just more work.

As young children, our parents helped us make friends by arranging play dates and get-togethers for us. They'd make friends with other adults who had kids the same age, and they'd throw us all together. Most kids also have an innate ability to make friends on their own; they connect with other kids in the neighborhood by virtue of the fact that they see one another every day, ride their bikes down the same street, and take the same bus to school. And little kids are brutally honest with their friends. A 6-year-old who gets angry at a kid in the schoolyard will say, "I hate you. I'm not your friend." There are a lot of broken little hearts in schoolyards.

As adolescents, we were still open enough to be somewhat honest about our feelings, so we didn't hesitate to ask some-one to "be our friend." We could also be very deliberate about shunning or dropping those we no longer wanted. At that age, forming and ending friendships was a process dictated purely by passion and style. When someone was no longer useful, we'd simply dump him or her unceremoniously.

But among adults, the game changes radically. We're required to be more strategic, and more *insincere* about why we choose certain friends, why we keep them, and how we dispose of them when they no longer fit. All adults play this game. It's part of how we survive.

I had a conversation with my parents recently about how

they felt about some of their senior citizen friends. They told me stories of couples in which one member was adored and the other despised, or friends whose personalities had become tiresome, whose eccentricities were no longer endearing, but downright irritating. And stories of friends who for one reason or another no longer had common interests with my parents, yet remained part of their social lives, even though being with them was dreaded and unpleasant. My parents' example mirrors all of us, because dealing with changes in the status of our friendships is an issue that everyone has to face. Making new friends—and leaving old ones behind as we grow and change—is a vital part of contact making and breaking.

Hollywood Friendships

The term *Hollywood friendships* will be immediately recognizable to anyone in the entertainment industry. The rest of you will also find it sadly familiar, because it describes a social phenomenon that affects all industries. It happens when the line between business acquaintances and true friends begins to blur—for a second. It happens when you start to think that your clients, your coworkers, and your associates are actual *friends*. And it happens to all of us, whether you're a trash-truck driver or a dancer with the American Ballet Theater.

In 1992, before Michael and I got together, the stress of his photojournalism career was beginning to take its toll, and Michael took a sabbatical from his hectic life. His was suffering from severe depression, his marriage had ended, and he recovered by fleeing the fast lane for a simpler existence in a small town in northern Arizona. When he returned to L.A. after 2 years, Michael had a whole new perspective on life. We had been together for about 6 months at that point, and we decided to throw a big party to celebrate his forty-third birthday, and to introduce each other to our respective groups of friends.

We started planning the party by going through Michael's database, which had about 3000 names in it. Each entry had a field in which Michael had labeled each person as a "friend" or "business" relationship. Of the 3000 names, he had identified about 750 as friends. As we went through the list, Michael took a long, hard look at who his real friends were. The 750 ended up being edited down to about 100. The remainder were dubbed "Hollywood friends." These were the ones Michael had worked with in the past, and had become friendly with during the course of a particular project. He'd been to their homes for Thanksgiving dinner, attended their kids' birthday parties, and thought of them as personal friends. But after the projects had faded into the past, the relationships faded too. Although Michael worked hard at staying in touch, he realized that it had always been *him* initiating the contacts. During the 2 years he'd been in Arizona, even though he'd sent correspondence to everyone announcing where he was, almost none called to see how he was doing.

Not long after this, we went to another party filled with dozens of Michael's old friends. Everybody was very happy to see him. They hugged and exchanged air kisses, and we all had a lovely time. But on the way home, that nagging feeling about Hollywood friendships started to set in. We talked about the people at the party, and Michael recounted the good times he'd shared with them at presidential inaugurations, Academy Awards parties, and film premieres. The more he talked, the more he realized that they were clients and business associates. Not really *friends*. All the way home, we worked on defining the meaning of a friend.

"A friend is someone you can sit around with in your underwear drinking beer and watching TV," I offered. "Do you have that kind of relationship with any of them?"

Michael thought about it and came up blank. Nobody at the party qualified.

"A friend is someone who calls just to say hello, and doesn't want anything from you," he postulated. "Someone who invites you to lunch for no reason other than to just hang out."

What a novel idea! So unlike most of the relationships we know of in the industry.

"So how many of the people in that room tonight meet that criterion?" I asked him.

"One. Maybe two."

"How many called you while you were in Arizona to see if you were OK?" I reminded him.

He thought hard about this one.

"None."

We've all experienced this in some form. It's great when you can be buddies with your clients and coworkers. But as soon as the business ends, so usually does the friendship. There's nothing wrong with that, of course, but be careful not to delude yourself. I remember once working with a rock & roll record producer who had many hits and a few Grammys, and was on top of the world at the time. He was in my office one day, and used my phone to call to a "friend" at one of the record companies. The receptionist put him on hold for a long time. While he waited, he looked at me and said, "See what happens when you don't have a record in the top 10?"

Friendships Between Couples

When my ex-husband, Jim, and I were first married, we were surprised to find that our interest in friends who were in romantic relationships *without commitments* had diminished. While we were oriented toward building a future with the assumption that we'd spend it together, it became awkward to spend time with couples who didn't know whether they'd still be together next week.

The same thing happened when we became parents. The number of childless couples within our circle dropped, and our typical evenings spent with friends changed style drastically. Dinner at 8:00 with fascinating individuals having deep intellectual conversations was replaced by backyard barbecues surrounded by plastic toys and talk about preschools and pediatricians. By 8:00 the party would be over, with weary parents packing up cranky kids and heading home for a vegetative evening in front of the television.

We realized that these changes were part of a very normal process, and that they were happening to everyone we knew. When some status in your life changes, you can be certain that your circle of friends is going to change too.

Couples can meet other couples in exactly the same way single people meet one another. Start talking to other couples in shopping malls, in line at the movie theater, or at the beach. Use eye contact, opening lines, and other conversational tips (see Chapter 2) in much the same way you would at a business function. When you meet an interesting couple that you'd like to know better, exchange phone numbers and suggest getting together sometime in the future. And then, do the work—follow up! Make it happen. Have a dinner party and invite two or three other new couples that you think might blend well.

Jim and I made a point of doing this all the time, because we were newly coupled and wanted to add friends to our new configuration. We'd have a dinner party about once a month, and invite couples that we'd recently met, mixing them with other friends and couples. Our parties were marvelous adventures, filled with stimulating conversation, humor, friendly debate, and lots of warmth. We experimented with mixing contrasting types in order to expand our social circle as well as our minds. (We once put together a group containing a Scientologist couple, a pair of born-again Christians, and a Jewish/Catholic couple because we wanted to have a conversation about different religious perspectives.) These parties led to dinner invitations at the other people's homes, and the beginnings of long-term friendships between those of us who really clicked. We loved our friends. They were an important part of our life.

When Jim and I split up 8 years later, we sent a final edition of our newsletter to our friends, announcing our separation. In the letter, we told everyone that it wasn't necessary for them to feel uncomfortable or to choose sides, that things were quite amicable between us, and that we both wanted to remain friends with all of them. It was an interesting experiment, because although it wasn't our intention, our friends' responses to the newsletter clearly showed the lines of demarcation: The people who wanted to stay friends with him, called him. The people who "chose" me, called me.

Friendships Between Single People

When you're part of a couple, you tend to be friends with other couples. The few exceptions, of course, are the single friends you're constantly trying to fix up so they can become couples too. But if you're part of a couple that breaks up, it's a whole new ball game when the friends start getting divided along with the community property. He gets Joe and Sara and Valerie and Rob, and she gets Eileen and Sam and Jane and Eric. He gets his perpetual adolescent pal Gary, a committed bachelor who'll soon be leading him around town reintroducing him to the single life, and she gets her lifelong friend Sandra, a neurotic 45-year-old who's decided to give up on finding a husband and is thinking about becoming a nun.

How do you find friends in the foreboding landscape of a new life? In a setting you've entered through separation from a partner, moving to a new city, or simply a desire to disconnect from old friends and cultivate new ones? You develop a plan of action—a marketing campaign for yourself designed to help you meet as many people as possible.

Start by joining organizations and clubs. Volunteer for community service organizations. Call everyone you have even the slightest connection with (even that nice daughter of the Greenbergs whom your mother told you to stop by and see if you're ever in Baltimore), and invite them all to pot lucks at your place every weekend. Socialize with people from your job. Get a dog (from the pound—have a heart!) and go to the park to meet other people with dogs. Take walks early on Sunday mornings and stop at your neighborhood coffee and croissant place to make friends with the regulars. Go to a self-improvement seminar—heal your emotional life and make new friends at the same time! Offer your professional services (free of charge) to charities, arts organizations, political causes, or anything else that interests you.

Then, follow up—big time. And remember the most important rule of all: *Tell the truth*. The more real you are about who you are and what you want, the better response you'll get from people. If you can say to someone, "I'm new in town, I just got divorced, and I'm trying to meet people and make friends," you'll be way ahead of the person who's trying to cover up and act like he's the coolest guy around when in fact he's so lonely he just wants to curl up in the fetal position and cry.

When people are lonely, they bond for different reasons from people who are surrounded by friends, families, and loved ones. When I was single, my friends and I chose each other because we were good at entertaining one another. We helped each other fill up the empty hours, and were there to talk to, to ask for advice, to share experiences, and to be each other's *family*.

But when one of them would find a mate, he or she would disappear because the mate provided that same kind of support. Some people may resent being replaced and subsequently ignored when their friends fall in love and don't have time for them anymore. But it isn't a matter of having time. It's a matter of refocusing energy, which is a natural part of developing new relationships.

A true friendship doesn't require its participants to stay exactly the same all the time. Instead, it allows them to grow and change. Friendships can survive a lifetime *if they're allowed to take different forms over the years*. In a sense, we're all fair-weather friends if you consider that our lives and our needs are constantly changing. What worked in a friendship between two single guys in college isn't going to work a few years later when one of them is married with two kids and the other is still going to bars trying to meet women.

But that doesn't mean the friendship has to die. It just has to *change*. So maybe instead of going out together every Friday night as they used to, the friends drift apart in a natural way, and see each other only on certain occasions, such as the kids' birthday parties, weddings, and an occasional get-together with old college friends.

I have three best friends who have endured with me forever, and I'm grateful that we've weathered so many changes together over the years. One is Rose, whom I've been close to since we were 7 years old. We were Beatle fans together in 1965. We were hippies together in 1972. Then she got married, moved to the suburbs, and had two kids, and there she's stayed ever since. I went off to live on hippie communes, be a writer, and develop a completely different view of the world. But we see each other once or twice a year, we talk on the phone every few months or so, and we always click right in to our life-long bond as if nothing had ever changed between us. Because the basics never have.

My very best lifetime friend in the world is Don, whom I've known since we were 15. He lives on a 25-acre ranch in northern California with his wife and young child. He's never worked at a job, and never had to worry about money (his wealth is inherited), which sets him apart from everyone else I know. He spends his days riding around his property on his tractor, tinkering with his inventions, and leisurely working in his home darkroom, where he produces stunningly beautiful photographs. By contrast, I live in Los Angeles and spend my days in rush-hour traffic on the freeway, schmoozing with clients and running three businesses, and working on my third marriage.

Don and I were very close during the 1970s, when we lived in the same northern California town. When I moved to Los Angeles in 1980 to seek fame and fortune, we could have easily drifted apart. But I made a point of staying in touch, visiting every year, calling, writing, and generally making sure that I didn't lose him, because he's one of the best people I've ever known. And so we've worked at maintaining our relationship for over 20 years. Our kids think of each other as cousins. We're family, and I proudly refer to him as my best friend, although on the surface, it would appear that we have nothing in common at all.

My other best friend is Shelley, a woman with whom I spent some of the wildest days of my counterculture youth. We met at a campground in Key West, Florida in 1974, when we were hard-core hippies. I had been hitchhiking around the country in search of myself, and she was an art student at a southern university. We ended up hitting the road together that summer, hitchhiking from Florida to the state of Washington, and we had amazing adventures that could fill up a book of their own.

In the fall she had to go back to school, and I returned to California. She moved to New Mexico after that, and then to Arizona, where she married Peter. They moved to Alaska and worked on fishing boats. She eventually divorced Peter and married Warren, who had four grown kids. She and Warren both own Harley-Davidson motorcycles, which they take on long trips across the country. Our lifestyles couldn't be more diverse, but we talk and write to each other all the time, and are as close as ever. We just took a trip to the Grand Canyon together after 5 years of not seeing one another, and it was as if we'd never been apart.

Through all these years, across dozens of states and a few countries, Shelley and Rose and Don have remained my best friends, for two reasons:

1. We allowed our relationships to change form.

2. We worked hard at staying in touch year after year.

Making friends may indeed be more work as we get older, but if we can learn how to make better contact with strangers, we'd have much better luck turning them into friends. We just have to be willing to do most of the work ourselves.

You and your spouse might have met an interesting couple during intermission at the ballet last month. You might even have exchanged phone numbers. But 9 times out of 10, *they* won't call *you*. People have busy lives, and the act of turning a stranger into a friend takes a lot of time and effort. If you really want somebody to be your friend, you have to pursue him in much the same way you'd pursue someone you want as a client or a mate. Friendships, like all relationships, need tender loving care. Once a friendship is established—once the seeds are planted—it requires constant nurturing to stay alive and healthy.

In Chapter 10 is some valuable information on how to stay in touch with new people you've met in your public and your private life. Try using some of those techniques combined with the following ideas for maintaining friendships.

*   *   *   *   *

How to Make and Keep New Friends

1. Host monthly or bimonthly dinner parties for six to eight in your home (or in a restaurant where each person pays his or her own way) and invite the new people you meet to mix and mingle with others. If you feel that you're not very good at being a gregarious host, ask one of your friends who has a more outgoing personality to be your partner in this project. You'll be amazed at the results.

2. Send a newsletter regularly to everyone you know and every new person you meet. Keep track of their names and addresses on a computer database.

3. Become involved in a political or community issue that you know will be of interest to your friends, and invite them to participate with you.

4. Make a point of getting together for lunch or dinner at least once a month with a friend.

5. Offer to trade professional services and other kinds of support with your friends. If your friend is a lawyer, offer to baby-sit for her kids in exchange for an hour of legal advice. If your friend is a carpenter, ask if he'll fix your broken stairs in exchange for an equal value of your services as a bookkeeper.

6. Start a tradition! Host a seasonal party to which all your friends are invited *each year.* Or conduct a charity drive every spring to collect used clothing for the needy. Create something that your friends will come to expect from you on a regular basis, like my New Year's Day party (going on its ninth year!).

7. Organize group events, like picnics on the beach or outings to a play. In my neighborhood, all the mothers on the block have a tradition called "The Moms' Dinner." Once a month we leave the kids at home with their dads or with baby-sitters, and we all go out to a nice restaurant for a long, leisurely dinner where we can spend time together without interruption.

*   *   *   *   *

Letting Go

Sometimes, very little changes on the outside while everything changes on the inside. What then? Sometimes we grow in ways that our friends can't fathom, and we're faced with the prospect of having to abandon them. Even the most subtle change in your psychology can be a catalyst for saying goodbye to friends who were part of the old you.

A good example of this is a person who's decided to put an end to excessive drinking, drug use, or other addictive behaviors. A major part of that transformation involves leaving old friends and enablers behind, and creating a new, healthier life. In addiction recovery you learn that it's not just the drug that keeps you plugged in, it's the culture that goes with the drug—the social atmosphere and the emotional environment that supported the lifestyle you've chosen to move beyond.

When we grow and change emotionally, what we have to give and what we need from others changes too. When we consciously change elements of our personalities, we often lose the people who were part of our old way of being, unless they happen to be growing in the same way. We all know of someone who's seen a long-term friendship end because of this kind of change.

For me, after 12 years of friendship with my best buddy Laura, she suddenly dropped me without explanation soon after I'd made some improvements in my life. I was really hurt by her sudden change of attitude toward me, and I called her and wrote her letters asking her to talk to me about it. But she never responded, and for years I wondered what happened. I even dropped off a bottle of champagne at her house one New Year's Eve, with a note saying, "I love you, please call me." I got no reply.

I finally concluded that after Laura and I had spent so long together as young, single women—flat broke, scraping by on odd jobs, partying and drinking, staying up all night smoking cigarettes and crying on each other's shoulders about the men who broke our hearts—we had become *bonded by that lifestyle.* Then one day my life changed. I wasn't so wild anymore. I was no longer poor. I stopped falling in love with men who treated me badly and found one who treated me like a queen. And despite my best efforts to stay close to Laura, she chose to disappear. Or maybe in some subconscious way, I chose to let her go.

That was 8 years ago. To this day I still send her Christmas cards and an occasional invitation to a party, but I never hear from her. She has since been replaced by countless other friends, none of whom live the kind of life Laura and I shared. Because as I've changed, so have the people who are drawn to me. Most of them have families and are financially stable. None of them are wasting their lives in relationships with an abusive partner. And none are dependent on drugs or alcohol.

I still don't know what it was about my new life that turned Laura off. She too had a new, improved life—she had married a wonderful man, stopped doing drugs, saw her children grow into confident, loving adults, and seemed to be quite happy. I wanted us to know each other in our new lives. She apparently didn't have the same vision. I still miss her and her rare insights, articulate conversation, musical talent, and other qualities. If only she had communicated with me about her feelings...

The point is, you create your friends in your own image. And when you change, *they* have to change too. For my parents' generation, the rules of polite behavior dictate that they should tolerate relationships with people they don't really like for the sake of politeness and appearance. So they complain about how they can't stand Ernie and his war stories another minute, and they hate Ernie's wife, who does nothing but complain to my mother in private about what a jerk Ernie is. Yet they play cards with Mr. and Mrs. Ernie every week and act like they're the best of friends, because they've known one another for so many years that they can't change anything now. It's scary to think about how many relationships in our lives—personal and professional—we might be conducting in the same manner.

We're afraid to let go of the friends and lovers we've out-grown because we think we'll never find replacements for them. But then, as time passes, we find out that it isn't so. We do eventually make new friends, but it doesn't happen auto-matically. It takes time and effort. We can speed up the process by following the principles of aggressive socializing and going at it tirelessly.

A Final Word

In the 6 years since the Power Schmoozing seminars began, I've received thousands of letters and phone calls from people who've experimented with the techniques and been amazed at the results. While on the surface it might seem that aggressive socializing is something only businesspeople need to do, the seminars regularly attract retired people, college kids, construction workers, artists, schoolteachers, stay-at-home moms, and even visitors from other countries. What is it they're looking for? Why would anyone sign up for a seminar with a ridiculous name like Power Schmoozing?

Because they're looking for a way to feel comfortable *being themselves*. Rarely, if ever, will you find that the new rules—*telling the truth, taking risks, telling your whole story*, and *breaking rules*—get you into trouble. On the contrary, they will make you feel *safer* around other people, and will launch you *into* the world, rather than keeping you in the dark while you wait for the world to come to you. The only trouble you may encounter is that things will start to change very quickly, and old habits, old friends, old excuses for why things aren't working, and old definitions of who you are begin to disappear.

What you'll have instead is a sense of belonging in the world, and an ability to move through life a little more fearlessly, a little more freely, and with a lot more confidence.

Good luck.

And *don't* be careful out there!

Resource List

Use the following resource list as a guide to help you find associations, clubs, events, and other activities that can help you make contact.

Directories of Events and Associations

Directory of Trade Shows   (312) 579-9090
Trade shows in a wide range of industries

Chase's Calendar of Events   (908) 665-2846
Interesting events throughout the United States

Encyclopedia of Associations   (313) 962-2242
Professional, cultural, political, and other associations

Association Meeting Directory   (800) 541-0663
Meetings of professional associations nationwide

U.S. Small Business Administration   (202) 653-6600
Ask for the number of the regional office in your town

Directories of Trade Magazines and Other Sources (Selected Examples)

Bacon's Publicity Checker   (312) 922-2400
Trade publications for all industries and special interests

Ad Lib Publications   (800) 669-0773
Media contacts, all areas of interest

The Hollywood Reporter Blue Book   (213) 525-2000
The definitive entertainment industry directory

Online Information Network	(402) 593-4593
On-line directories for businesses	
Encyclopedia of Business Information Sources	(313) 962-2242
Encyclopedia of Senior Citizen Resources	(313) 962-2242

Selected Regional Calendars and Directories

You can call the Convention and Visitors Bureaus (CVBs) in any city in the United States to ask if they publish a local events directory or calendar of events. Most large cities (and some small ones) have them. Here are a few examples:

Los Angeles Master Planner	(310) 888-8568
Metro Milwaukee Calendar of Events	(800) 231-0903
Miami Calendar of Events	(305) 375-4634
Phoenix Area Calendar of Events	(602) 254-6500
San Antonio Events Calendar	(800) 447-3372
Seattle Calendar of Events	(206) 461-5840

CVBs can also provide you with the names of local business trade groups, charities, arts associations, and other organizations that offer excellent networking opportunities.

Volunteering

The following organizations were chosen because they offer unique networking opportunities through *volunteering*. These listings cover a very wide range of interests, to illustrate the point that by becoming involved in groups such as these you'll be able to meet people of like mind who share your affinities and concerns.

Most of these groups host fund-raising events, meetings, and other types of gatherings ranging from low-priced get-togethers like bowling tournaments to elaborate black-tie affairs with celebrities. Others may have a lower profile.

While I chose groups for this section according to my personal affinities, it wasn't possible for me to thoroughly investigate the work of each group, so this list does not necessarily constitute a recommendation. But these are the *types* of groups that attract widely diverse and interesting people. For more information on finding groups that relate to your business or personal interests, refer to Chapter 1, or consult the *Encyclopedia of Associations,* which can be found at your local library.

Volunteering your time to support groups such as these not only helps you further the causes you believe in, but also helps you build a circle of contacts that can last a lifetime. These organizations do everything from AIDS research to raising funds to support avant-garde artists.

In addition to these nationally focused groups, check your local newspapers for events sponsored by local museums, hospitals and clinics, ecological groups, schools, community centers, theaters, historical societies, animal advocacies, women's and children's services, arts foundations, and political movements. You'll find no shortage of involvement opportunities, and social events to go along with them.

Most of the phone numbers listed here are for the organization's *national headquarters.* Call to find chapters in your area. If you find that any of these numbers are outdated, call 800 directory assistance at (800) 555-1212 to get the current number, or simply keep abreast of local and national news to learn about other organizations.

Organizations Offering Opportunities to Make Contact Through Volunteering

American Cancer Society
(404) 320-3333
Raises funds for cancer research

American Foundation for Performing Arts
(310) 859-7689
Raises funds and support for various causes

American Film Institute
(213) 856-7600
Supports the work of aspiring filmmakers
American Foundation for AIDS Research (AMFAR)
(800) 458-5231
Raises funds for AIDS research
American Senior Citizens Association
(919) 323-3641
Helps seniors stay active, socialized, and involved
Amnesty International
(800) 266-3789
Works to free political prisoners worldwide
Business Volunteers for Arts
(212) 819-9277
Business professionals donate services for arts organizations
City of Hope
(800) 275-1587
Research and programs for disabled children
Childhelp USA
(800) 422-4453
Information and referrals for child abuse victims
Comic Relief
(800) 528-1000
Raises money to help the homeless
Earth First
(602) 622-1372
Radical environmentalists to save the planet
Entertainment Industry Council on Substance Abuse
(703) 481-1414
Celebrities in support of antidrug programs and events
Fatherhood Project
(212) 268-4848
In support of fathers learning to be more nurturing
International Concerns for Children
(303) 494-8333
Arranges adoptions of foreign children
Make a Wish Foundation
(800) 332-9474
Fulfills wishes for children with terminal illnesses

March of Dimes
(914) 428-7100
Research and programs for children with birth defects

National Coalition on the Homeless
(202) 265-2371
Programs and other support for the homeless

National Council on Alcoholism and Drug Dependency
(800) 322-5245
Provides support and information

National Gay and Lesbian Task Force
(202) 332-6483
Support for gays and lesbians nationwide

National Multiple Sclerosis Society
(800) 458-9255
Fund-raising for MS research

National Women's Political Caucus
(800) 729-6971
Supports environmental and other political issues

Parents Without Partners
(800) 637-7974
Opportunities for single parents to meet and socialize

Pediatric AIDS Foundation
(800) 488-5000
Research and services for children with AIDS

People for Ethical Treatment of Animals
(301) 770-7444
Protects animals from abuse and exploitation

Planned Parenthood
(800) 830-2578
Provides birth control information and family counseling

Second Harvest
(312) 263-2303
Distributes food to food banks around the United States

S.H.A.RE. Inc.
(310) 476-4786
Helps disabled and abused children

20/20 Vision
(413) 549-4555
Organizes letter-writing campaigns to Congress in support of environmental and antiwar efforts

If you would like to be on the Power Schmoozing mailing list, or receive announcements of seminars and other events, please fill out this form and mail or fax it to:

Power Schmoozing
11288 Ventura Blvd. #392B
Studio City, CA 91604
Tel: (818) 980-0212
Fax: (818) 980-0289

Name: _____

Company: _____

Address: _____

City/State/ZIP: _____

Phone: (   ) _____

How did you hear about *Power Schmoozing?* _____

_____

_____

_____

Where did you purchase this book? _____

Store/source:_____

City/State: _____

Comments: _____

_____

_____

_____

_____

About the Author

Terri Mandell, an expert on communication and modern etiquette, is one of the top publicity consultants in Hollywood. Her nationally acclaimed Power Schmoozing seminars have attracted professionals in industries ranging from rock & roll to real estate. A successful journalist, she contributes frequently to such publications as *USA Today* and *Ladies Home Journal* and is the author of *When Good People Throw Bad Parties*. She lives in Los Angeles.